I'M SAD AND I NEED CAKE

WHEN REAL PEOPLE WRITE REAL LETTERS ABOUT GRIEF

Hannah Boland & Cecily Paterson

ABOUT THE AUTHORS

Hannah Boland is an Australian wife and mother to two living children. Born and raised in Melbourne, she grew up in a Christian household with her dad, mum, and sister. In her early teens she walked away from Christianity and did not return to God until after she was married.

Her husband, Michael, has also come to faith in Jesus Christ. They now enjoy raising their two children to the glory of God and are eager to see the purposes of God fulfilled in the lives of all their family members.

In 2011, with her three year old daughter Allison and her two year old son Harry in tow, Hannah was expecting their son Stephen. At the 20 week scan, she and Michael were informed by doctors that their son suffered from a rare brain abnormality known as Alobar Holoprosencephaly, meaning that most of Stephen's brain had failed to develop. It was unlikely that Stephen would live for very long if he was even to be born alive.

Hannah and Michael had to fight for Stephen's life right up until the very moment he was born, as doctors were determined to see them terminate the pregnancy. Stephen spent 47 hours with his parents before he was taken to heaven. Hannah writes about this heartbreaking journey in her first book, *47 Hours with a Prince*.

In January 2013, Hannah and Michael were expecting their rainbow baby, Esther Clare. Esther was a perfectly healthy baby and an eagerly anticipated arrival, especially for

Hannah's other children. Devastatingly, a routine check-up at the 36 week mark revealed that Esther had passed away. It was later discovered she had been asphyxiated by the umbilical cord, and she was born sleeping on the 22nd of January 2013.

This book began about one month later.

Cecily Paterson has an early memory of being hit by a wall of heat as she disembarked with her missionary family, blinking and dazed, from a flight landing in Karachi. She spent 13 dusty, colourful years in the city, desert and mountain landscapes of Pakistan and loved every minute. It was one of the biggest challenges of her life to leave her adopted home and return permanently to Australia at the age of 16.

Having eventually become used to Aussie life, she now resides happily in small town New South Wales with her husband and four children, one of whom lives with Autism Spectrum Disorder. Her current challenges are less exotic and involve many more dirty dishes, but they still take all the time, energy and problem-solving abilities she has.

Cecily and Hannah met when Hannah read *Love Tears & Autism,* Cecily's award-winning memoir about the four years following her son's diagnosis with ASD. Hannah contacted Cecily with some questions about her own book and discovered that they both had friends in common.

Having been through depression, grief and chronic, unrelenting stress, and having (mostly) come out the other side, Cecily has found herself to be much more empathic, much less judgmental and much more open to people's stories than she was before. While she wouldn't choose Autism Spectrum Disorder for her son, she agrees (sometimes through gritted teeth) that the whole family has received other, unexpected blessings from their ASD journey.

Cecily is trying to fulfill her childhood dream of being a real, actual fiction writer, focusing on young teenage girls. She's currently working on her third novel.

- 1 -

Dear Cecily,

I've been thinking about this project idea for quite a few months now. The trouble was, a few months ago when I started thinking about writing letters to a friend that I could share with everyone (provided that our letters don't end up being utter unintelligible crap that no one else can understand, which I'm not ruling out at this point), the concept never got any further than my brain because I realised that I really had nothing to write about. Life was on track (whatever I thought that meant). And besides, I would be far too busy and tired with a new-born baby to focus on any sort of writing. Maybe the Lord would give me something meaty in his timing, you know—down the track.

The sentiment 'be careful what you pray for' comes to my mind.

So, here I am. This week I find myself having one of the most miserable weeks of my life. Michael has gone back to work after four weeks of carer's leave since Esther was born. I find myself unable to be at home by myself on the days when the kids are both at school because the house is so empty. There is supposed to be a baby crying for my attention, needing a feed or a nappy change, and I should be scrambling for naps in between all of these things. Instead I find myself sitting in a chair, my mind unable to focus on any one thing, my body too tired and emotionally exhausted to begin any sort of purposeful or useful activity, my hands trembling slightly from all of the stress, and then the anxiety begins. It's truly awful.

Adding to the awfulness of this week is the fact that about six of my friends who were all expecting babies around the same time as me are having their babies. It seems that every time I log onto Facebook there is another picture of a freshly born child with their beaming mum. I am truly happy for each of my friends and their families, but the hurt is almost unbearable. I feel like some people would just suggest not to go onto Facebook for a while, but I think that would be more difficult for me as it's one of the ways I am able to keep in contact and be supported by my friends at the moment.

Tomorrow is also looming heavily in my mind. Tomorrow is the 1st of March; the date when Esther was scheduled to be born via c-section. I am dreading it. I am also surprised and a little hurt that none of my close friends seem to register what week it is. In fairness, I don't know that I actually told many people about the scheduled date, yet my friends knew that she was due to be born in the first week of March and that the c-section was to be scheduled one week prior. I am trying very hard not to have unfair expectations on my friends, but I can't help but feel like this is a bloody big oversight, and it's hurt on top of a lot of other hurt at the moment.

To be honest, that is probably the thing that is upsetting me the most this week. It's the recognition that friendships change, not all valued friendships are going to meet every need, the friends who I really need to be there for me the most are not there, and that I am a hypocrite because if the roles were reversed I would probably be guilty of the same thing. Sadly, I feel like I learned a lot of this when I lost Stephen. I suppose the fact that I know it does not take away from how much the reality hurts.

After Stephen died I went through a long period of time where I closely examined the friendships and relationships in my life, and realised that we do tend to place a lot of expectations on people that are probably quite unfair. It also highlighted to me that many of our relationships and friendships are not viewed the same way by both parties i.e. one friend may view a friendship as being extremely close and rich with meaning, where as the other half of that same relationship may deem their friend as 'fun to be around' and not much more.

This reality is hurtful beyond belief at the moment, especially with the world of pain I am in. The people whom I trust the most (and there are only very few) with the inner most secrets and emotions of my being are the ones who are too busy to fit me in to their schedule or are so unsure of how to respond to my pain that they avoid the topic all together.

Frankly, I feel like a bit of a cow really. There are so many other people in my life who are more than willing to make time for me, to listen to me and to share my pain with me, and I appreciate them all. In fact, I met a young mum the other week who bluntly admitted that she had no friends at all. She is a lady who lost her baby roughly half way through her pregnancy, and when I asked her how she coped with that loss without any friends, she replied, "that's what social workers are for."

So I know I have no right to complain. There are many people who love and care for me dearly. It's just that it takes so many years to build a deep mutual trust with a person where I feel I can let them into the inner circle of my grief without being judged, without being clichéd to death, and without needing to make an appointment with them two weeks in advance. Then there's the trump card of being a good listener—a subject that I know you have learned a lot about over time, probably out of necessity as I have.

You see, when I first moved out of home and was finally living and working as an independent 'adult', I remember becoming hugely frustrated that people wouldn't 'hear' me. At work, with friends or at home—everyone seemed to cut me off mid-sentence and it drove me insane! When I noticed that everyone was doing it I began to feel very down about myself as I had concluded that nobody really valued me or what I had to say about anything. No one would even give me the courtesy of finishing a sentence. That was until I started to listen to what was coming out of my own mouth. I soon realised that I was doing exactly the same thing to others; even to people whom I deeply cared about and valued their opinion. They would start to say something and I would have to butt in with the memory that it had just triggered in me, or my particular opinion on a subject.

From that realisation onward I have tried (and not nearly succeeded) to be a good listener; to allow the person speaking to me to finish their sentence, and to reflect and give time to what they have just said. Ironically, I thought I was getting quite good at this until I began studying for a Counselling qualification last year and realised that my listening skills still have a very long way to go. But it also highlighted to me that there are very, very few good listeners in our culture. Scarce as hens teeth one might say. But the ones who are absolute gems.

Which brings me back to my earlier topic of friends and expectations. Knowing full well that there are actually very few good listeners around, as well as the fact that people do have busy schedules and responsibilities (and good listening does take time—lots of it), I find myself reflecting on a key question about friendship that I don't know that I have an answer to. When someone is in a world of pain, in a genuine need, is it fair for that person to have the expectation on their close friends to drop everything, clear some time in their schedule and just listen? Is it okay for them to feel hurt if that doesn't happen? I'm not talking about people considered to be acquaintances or even just friends; I mean the people who we hold dearest. And I'm also not talking about chats until 3am every night, or neglecting families or jobs at the expense of a friendship, but I'm certainly talking about some sort of sacrifice. Is it right for me to expect this of my dearest friends? Is it right for my dearest friends to expect this from me? You've written a book about friendship—I'd love to know your thoughts about this.

As I mentioned earlier, these questions not only hurt me at the moment because I am feeling a little let down by my friends, they're also hurting because I really do have to face the question, "am I any different?" and I don't like the pain of that answer. It's too much hurt on top of everything else at the moment, and I just need to be selfish. Oh please Cecily, say I can be selfish. If I hadn't just lost a second baby and enduring more grief than I thought I could bear I may be able to face that with honesty. But surely not now.

You know, the thing is that as I am typing this and considering it, I just sense God being a little firm with me. I very much have a sense of his love and gentleness with me at the moment, but also his fatherly touch that reminds me that his love and mercy and grace still does not mean that he will tolerate my sin once he has convicted me of it. I hate the fact that when I am down for the count emotionally I still have to recognise that I am a sinner. Insert audible sigh here.

There's another thing that I have given much consideration to over these past months; the western 'church' (stay with me, it's related). It seems to me that in our culture there is a huge premium on academia and intellect that it has woven its way into our church. For some reason we tend to only pay attention (well as much as we pay

13

attention to anything) if the person giving the teaching or the mentoring is qualified to do so. We want people who have degrees and doctorates so that we know what they are preaching is 'good'. We want sermons and bible studies to challenge us in new ways, to educate us, to stimulate our intellect, and I think we mislabel this as the 'meat' as opposed to the 'milk' that Peter talks about in 1 Peter 2:1-3. We think that if we can be more intellectual about God's word that it will somehow draw us closer to him; that if we can study it more and apply more of our theories and theology that it will somehow make us better Christians. Then I think about the Christians in China who don't have bibles to read and often don't have formal teaching. Does God love them less? Do they know God less?

It has been an issue I have thought about deeply. And please don't misunderstand what I am saying; I think it is good to have teaching from people who have studied God's word in a formal sense, and it is good to study God's word ourselves and to dig deeper. We should not abuse the privilege of freedom in our country to do so, and God will use it to grow and challenge and change us. It is his word after all. But I think we make a grave mistake if we consider it to be the only way in which we can know God more or even 'best'.

I will make a confession to you that I have not made to many people because of fear of judgement. But I'm going to put it out there. I've not picked up my bible and read it much in the past two years. Gasp. I know. Shocking. Yet the truth is that I have learned more about God and grown deeper in my relationship with him over the past two years than what I did for the four years prior, studying and reading my bible every day.

You can probably see why I am reluctant to admit this to anyone. It's not because I have made a deliberate decision not to read my bible every day. It's not because I think that reading my bible is unimportant. By no means. I have missed it and longed to be able to read it. Yet the trauma of the past two years has been so severe upon me mentally that I have struggled to keep the focus I have needed even just to read short passages, and on the occasions I managed to absorb things, all I could do was to sit and cry. There was no prayer time. There was no evident growth time. There were just tears.

I don't tell this to people because I don't like either of the two likely responses. The first is the judgement that I can't possibly be close to God if I'm not reading my bible and that I can't possibly be 'on track' in my relationship with him (whatever that means). The second is the get-out-of-jail-free card that some people would see this revelation as—an excuse not to read their bible.

It still grates against me in some way having to admit that I haven't read my bible much. I long to be able to do it and to spend that special time with God, which is the only reason I know that my not doing it is okay with him. For the moment at least. God has been so gracious to me, Cecily, it brings tears to my eyes now just to type it. He has met me where I have been at. He has comforted me through songs, he has been present with me in the embraces and love of my friends, and he has spoken to and taught me in the shower and in the car (the two times my thoughts are usually uninterrupted. You have children, so I know you understand exactly what I mean). It has not been intellectual 'meaty' teaching that has helped me to grow and to know him better, it has been obedience. Small, shaky, humble obedience. Every day that I decide to leave my ego at home and just to get on and love others and live my life in the way I know he expects, that is when the growth happens. That is when he reveals something of himself to me. Oh how I wish we would leave the intellectual bull-tish behind!

So, after being extremely upset from a recent meeting with a friend of mine who spent two hours having coffee with me and not asking me once how I was, I realise I have come to the end of a four page letter and not actually asked how you are. So how are you, Cecily? I would love to know. And I will do my very best to listen without interrupting and give you as much time as you need to tell me what's on your mind.

With love,

Hannah

-2-

Dear Hannah,

I have been trying to imagine myself with no baby in my arms after preparing for one for so long and it's terrible. I can imagine what the anxiety and shock must be like, especially with the older children off at school.

Sometimes, when you experience a terrible crisis, you can get through the main part of it, perhaps because of adrenaline, or just because you have to. It's what happens afterwards that is almost harder—the recovery period that seems chronic and never-ending.

I've had surgery a couple of times and each time I have been surprised at how long my body takes to get over it, even when it is something I think of as minor. But people have told me, "Well, your body has had a shock and it takes time to get over it," so I've sat still on the couch and waited until I felt better. I think sometimes we're a lot more forgiving about the recovery times for physical shock than emotional trauma.

You mentioned some of your friends having babies at the moment—around the same due date as Esther's. It is possible to be happy for someone, but yet hurt terribly at the same time. And I think it's pretty normal to want to stay away. When my little boy Cameron was diagnosed with ASD I stayed away from playgroup full stop. It wasn't that the people weren't nice (they were), it was just that I was jealous and sad because the biggest problems they seemed to face with their children were getting them to eat solids and which method to use to toilet train—star charts or pants off? My son's issues were a whole lot bigger than that and it was hard to join in the conversation without bursting into tears.

You talk about having unfair expectations of your friends—that you think they ought to have remembered Esther's due date and have realized that this was an important and difficult time for you.

Being a person who can't really think until she puts words on a page, for me it would be a helpful exercise to write down exactly what expectations you have of each individual you're talking about. But then add in what it is you're hoping to get from your expectation—what your need is. And then maybe you could think about other ways to meet the need. Perhaps using headings like this:

- ✐ Who are the people in my life I have expectations of?
- ✐ What exactly are my expectations of them?
- ✐ How would I feel if my expectation (need) was fulfilled?
- ✐ Where else can I fulfill this need?

I'm inclined to think that your anger is coming from the *unmet need* rather than from your friends' forgetfulness or apparent lack of care. I went through a stage last year where at every point I felt angry or low or frustrated I asked myself, "What do I need in this situation?" Often, it wasn't what I thought.

For example, at one point I had to take some paperwork to Medicare to get a refund for a particular appointment for one of my children. It had been quite a big deal for me to get the appointment, do the paperwork and then get myself up to the Medicare place to take care of it all. It involved quite a lot of organization and arrangements and I was very pleased with myself for doing it all on time and efficiently. Unfortunately however, the date on the receipt was wrong and the Medicare woman couldn't process it and give me the cash. I got much more shirty than I needed to and stormed out. When I finally started to cool down, my patient husband said, "What do you need in this situation?" and I had to think about it. It wasn't the cash (although that would have been nice). It was more that I needed validation and appreciation of my hard work and efforts in going the extra mile for my kids. I wanted someone to pat me on the back and say, "You're a good mum."

Anyway, the point is this: I wonder if your anger at your friends is actually some of your grief and pain being redirected. It's somehow easier to say, "My friends have wronged me," than it is to say, "I feel sad and low and terrible and it all really hurts." It can be easier to blame others than to sit with hard feelings.

Maybe this sounds harsh. I don't want you to go away and beat yourself up about it. You talk about perhaps being selfish and God being 'firm' with you, but that sounds unnecessarily hard, with a lot of excess guilt. I don't want you to think God is punishing you, but instead, loving and helping you.

Imagine how you would treat one of your children if they fell over on concrete and banged their lip or grazed their knee. You'd grab them and cuddle them immediately. Then you'd start to look at the ouchie and see what you needed to do to fix it up. You'd speak kindly to them while you cleaned and bandaged them. And you'd help them to put the whole thing into perspective and teach them how to speak about their feelings, but gently. You wouldn't be cross with them if they started to blame, for example, their brother (as happens in our house), or the concrete. You'd just redirect them to be more accurate about what's going on. Let's play pretend:

Child: "Yeeeeoowww. Ow, ow, ow, ow, ow."

Mother: "Oh, it hurts. It hurts a lot. I can see it's bleeding. Can I take a look?"

Child: "It hurts! Silly concrete. It's the step's fault. It shouldn't have been there."

Mother: "Sometimes we fall down steps. It happens. Now I'm going to clean the blood, okay?"

Child: "Okay.. sniff, sniff."

Mother: "How do you feel?"

Child: "I'm mad with the steps. I didn't want to fall."

Mother: "Sometimes we fall down steps and it hurts. But the step didn't do it. You can say, 'I feel sad because I don't like having an ouchie.'"

Child: "I feel sad because I don't like having an ouchie."

Mother: "What do you need to help you feel better?"

Child: "An ice block?"

Mother: "Okay, let's see if we have one."

I prefer to think of God in this role when I'm in pain. He knows what we need, and he gently redirects us to better ways of thinking so that we can have a clearer perspective on what's going on.

Having said all of that, I spent quite a bit of time thinking this week about friends and expectations. It was intriguing for me to realize that I put almost zero expectations on my friends. For anything really. I don't *expect* that anyone is going to hear me, care for me, care about me, take time out of their schedule for me, understand me or spend time with me. Of course, I invite people to do these things and lots of people *do* it and I really enjoy it when they do, but I don't think I expect them to. In fact, it's much more of a 'wow, really?' type reaction when someone does something nice for me. (Family is probably a different story, but we're not talking about that.)

Having zero expectations of my friends may save me from disappointment, but I'm not so sure that it's any more healthy than having overly high expectations. My attitude springs from what they call a 'third culture kid' childhood. I grew up as a child of expatriate parents in Pakistan. I wasn't 'Aussie' because we weren't living in the Australian culture, but I wasn't Pakistani either. I fit into a 'third culture' of expatriates living abroad. My friendships were for the most part short-lived. People came and went and it was rare to be friends with someone for more than a couple of years. That was the first thing.

The second came from boarding school. It's a bit complicated. From the age of six I was 'best friends' with a girl called Sarah. We were BFFs from afar. She lived three hours away from us and we saw each other a couple of times a year only. But they were great, great, great times. We wrote letters to each other in between. When we were both nine, Sarah went off to boarding school. I knew that I was going to the same school when I was eleven and I couldn't wait to join my best friend there.

Unfortunately it didn't work out that way. In the two years I had to wait, Sarah buddied up with another girl and when I arrived on the scene, ready to claim my friend, the other girl wasn't very happy about it. She did what eleven year old girls do best and made my life as miserable as possible. I was dumped, and then I was mistreated and bullied. It was the worst year of my life.

During this year and the next couple of years my unconscious thoughts were: "I am boring; no one wants to hear what I've got to say. People only really put up with me because they have to. I don't have any real friends. I can't take a joke. I'm not likeable."

My conscious thoughts became, "I don't actually need anyone, because they just let you down anyway."

I still wanted friends though so I set out to work out how to get them. It seemed obvious that everyone liked the people who were good listeners, so I began to develop that skill. I became good at allowing people to talk and agreeing and saying, "yes, well, what do you think about that?" and, "oh really?" and letting them go on and on.

To be honest, though, it became quite boring because it was all one-sided. I was the one doing all the listening and they were the ones doing all the talking so I had this duality playing out; on the one hand I knew no one would like me if I didn't listen to them, but when they never stopped to listen to me, I realized I didn't actually like them anyway.

These days, I still do a lot of listening, but things are mostly a lot more mutual, thankfully. Occasionally, though, I meet someone who appears to be an excellent listener. They ask me all sorts of questions and they appear really genuinely interested in the answers. At that point, I get nervous. *Are they really interested? If so, why? Or are they just pretending?* I can hear myself actively changing the subject and getting it back onto them when this happens and I have to work to calm down and not get flighty or overstressed.

In any conversation I have, I mostly appear comfortable (I think) but I'm always working out the balance: *Have I talked too much? Do I need to stop now? Should I shift the focus so it's more mutual?* It gets tiring and I don't last very long.

So, in summary, I have hardly any expectations of my friends. But I have a *lot* of expectations of myself. I'm guessing they're mostly unreasonable and irrational but that's probably another whole topic for another day.

But back to you. Part of the pain of pain is knowing that you're alone in it, that even if your friends *did* come and *did* support you and *did* remember all the right dates and say the right things, that they'd eventually all go home and you would be left alone with your pain. Just you, and the burden you carry.

Pain is pain because it hurts. And I don't really think that other people can help with that—much. Yes, we can do things here and there to ease the burden, and to let you know you're loved, but in the end, our pain is ours and ours alone. Only God will help carry it in the end.

Until your friends have suffered a little bit like you, they *can't* know and they won't be able to meet whatever expectations you have for them. It's too hard for them. You have to have been in a pit yourself to be able to help another person out of their own.

When I heard you'd lost Esther, I told an older lady at our church because I knew she had lost three babies in her younger years. Three weeks later she asked after you: "How is your friend doing? I've been praying for her." She'd been there. She knew the pain. Those are the people who are going to be able to help the most.

Anytime we have expectations of people, we can be assured that we will be disappointed at some stage. We have to let others be free to act how they act, because God gives us that freedom. Of course, we can protect ourselves against excessive strain or heartbreak by being careful about where we go and who we talk to when we're grieving, but that's probably another thing we can only really learn from experience.

I had more to write but I'm up to the fourth page, so I might let it be. I will, however, answer your final question, which was; 'how are you?' Because I don't want to bore you (and I know, yes, you asked, so you're not going to be bored, but it's hard to shift that mindset) I'll give you some bullet points.

I am:

• Always obsessed with my goal to be a successful teen fiction writer and generalized blogger. This is with me morning to night. It shapes my day and sets my priorities. I could talk for hours about this, but I don't.

• Overwhelmed by the food needs in my family with children with diagnosed intolerances and the need to cook everything they eat now that they can't really eat from packets. I'm tired, but I'm pleased with my new kitchen gadget (a Thermomix™) and I'm very pleased with my step by step approach to making it all happen.

• Enjoying working with other people doing stuff for our school P&C. Give me a task and I can Get. It. Done. Yeah.

• Trying to take care of myself in small ways by staying fit, lying down when I need to and not saying no to the occasional cupcake.

• Feeling slightly bad for not being more in touch with friends, now that I've read your letter and written this one.

• Slightly self-conscious about being considered 'bossy' or a 'strong character' after something someone said this week. It's true. I am, but it's not how I see myself at all. Actually I think I'm mostly a fence sitter and a fairly incompetent leader. Self-image is tricky.

And speaking of that, I realize that this letter might be coming across as bossy. Or even patronizing. Kind of a 'you've got this problem and I can fix it' approach. I've just re-read it and most of it is advice directed *at* you. Perhaps I haven't done much listening at all. Perhaps I haven't given you permission to say what you wanted to say and just let it sit there in the air between us.

To tell the truth, I'm actually pretty nervous about sending this letter. I can see its flaws. I can see my flaws too. And I can see my own inexperience. I mean, what are you supposed to say to someone who's lost two babies and organized two funerals in two years? Will you hate me? Will you think I'm an unsympathetic know-it-all who only wants to fix things?

In all honesty, being a problem solver is probably my default position. It's the way I approach my own life, and more often than not, the way I approach other people's lives. It helps me avoid uncertainty and helps me get things right. But perhaps that whole approach is based on being afraid. Maybe I've written this letter out of fear, trying to get it 'right' so that you (and others, possibly) won't criticize me. Perhaps that's what I'm most scared of—the fear of judgment.

Cecily x

-3-

Dear Cecily,

I have a confession to make. When we talked about writing these letters initially I made such a point about being able to take our time to consider a response and not feeling rushed. Yet as soon as I pressed 'send' on my last letter I was so eager to get your response that I could not stop thinking about it. I was so pleased to receive your letter and I have read it many times already.

I sort of feel like we have a little secret, you and I. Not many people know that you and I don't know each other very well, and meeting you at Esther's funeral six weeks ago was only the second time I have met you in person in my life! The first time I ever heard of Cecily Paterson was when a friend of mine 'liked' your Facebook page for your book *Love, Tears*

& *Autism* almost two years ago. I decided to buy a copy and I remember reading it all in one sitting because I loved it so much. I also remember contacting you not long after I had finished reading it because I thought you seemed like an approachable character and I wanted some advice about publishing my own story. I had no idea when I made that first contact with you that we lived relatively close to each other, knew a lot of the same people and had both been a part of the same congregation, albeit at different times.

So I am so pleased to be writing to you and getting to know you more. It also amuses me greatly that we are both going to such pains to not offend each other by performing the dance of caution that is necessary when building a new friendship. It is often an unspoken dance, sometimes even unconsciously performed, yet I am acutely aware of it as I review the substance of our friendship to date in print in the full knowledge that one day our letters, confessions and little secrets may well be read by others. Talk about pressure to get it right!

It's funny. I had convinced myself that I had no expectation of what I thought your reply to my last letter should be. Who am I to tell you how to reply? Yet as soon as I got your letter I realised that it was not what I had expected. Sorry. Mark one fail to me. Or even maybe two; one for having an expectation and two for having the gall to rate you against it. Actually, that should probably be three. A third one for convincing myself that I didn't have an expectation to start with. On second thoughts, perhaps we shouldn't keep score. I think I am going to come off second best here.

After the grief I have journeyed through during the past two years of my life, I suppose I am so used to being patted on the head, stroked on the back and told that it is okay to feel whatever I am feeling that it was out of the ordinary for me to have someone actually tell me what they think even if it risked a little upset. I don't think a sweeping statement about either your approach or my expectation would be accurate or helpful here. Admittedly, I do feel a little frustration at being confronted with the idea that I need to sit and re-evaluate my expectations and assess my friendships, and not because you confronted me with it. It's the reality that I have to be considering these things at such a time that frustrates me. This is not a time in my life where I need to be assessing my friendships; it's the time I need to be enjoying them and leaning on them.

I can see that you are anxious about not upsetting me and saying the right thing. But as with most things, it's not about what is said exactly; it is the intent behind it. It is true that many people say things that are hurtful and unhelpful during times of extreme emotional stress and grief. But as a grieving person and as a friend, I do think *that* would be an awfully unfair expectation to have on people; to say the right thing all of the time. If a grieving person wants to avoid being totally shattered during a time of sorrow, I believe they must take it upon themselves to look past the actual words and try to see the heart of the person. Sometimes this can cause pain as many kind words can be spoken with a hurtful intent or gross inaccuracy. Equally, a person who is just plain thoughtless or tries to offer something kind which accidentally comes out 'wrong' does not necessarily need to be chastised. Nor should the recipient take offense. My goodness, could you imagine how much trouble we would be in if God always judged us by the words that came out of our mouths rather than the intention of our hearts, especially during the times we are genuinely trying to do good? I've muffed it so many times in my life that I'm ashamed.

I have a friend who said to me some months after Stephen died that she hardly ever mentioned Stephen because she was terrified of saying the wrong thing, and even after the few things she did say she had panicked, afraid she had hurt me. I had to spend some time assuring her that even if she had said anything which had upset me (not that I could even remember such an instance), I was never worried about it because I knew the heart of my friend; she was someone who loved and cared for me, and was only eager to help me in my trials.

It is in this vein Cecily, that I have read your letter. Aside from the admission of our little secret, I know enough of your character from your writings, your reputation amongst people who know you personally and from my experience of you to know that you are a genuine, kind and loving woman who loves Jesus. You mean no harm in what you say, in fact you mean just the opposite—you mean to show me love and to help. What more could I ask for? May I lovingly suggest that you afford yourself some of the grace you are willing to extend towards others who don't know how to help.

So I have been thinking particularly deeply about the section you wrote about friendship and expectations. And yes, to be honest, when I first read it I balked. I immediately thought *that's not me, she's got it all wrong*. Admittedly, this is a big fault of mine. I have a habit of reading or listening to someone (especially when it is an observation made about me) and analysing the content in a nanosecond to the point where I feel I can determine whether or not it applies to me. I reject and move on very quickly, which hardly ever allows opportunity for people to speak into my life or for me to consider something new. I learned this about myself after many sessions with my psychologist last year; she would say something that would grate against me badly and make me feel that she had it so wrong that it really didn't apply to me and my situation. Yet in the days to follow, as I reflected upon the situations we had been discussing and had a few 'goes' at sorting things out mentally, I don't think there was one time when I didn't have to admit that she had a point. She was, in fact, spot on. So I had to force myself not to respond instantly to your letter and to mull over its contents for a few days. And I'm so glad I did.

I have been trying to pin-point what the need is that I feel some friends have failed to meet. Everything I came up with just sounded superficial. You are so right—it is not about remembering dates or details, and deep down I always knew that. So what is it that has been upsetting me so much?

I remember a piece you wrote some time ago on your blog about being heard. You described a day-trip you took with your husband on which you ended up having a disagreement for a good portion of the day. You expressed how frustrated you were, and as you pondered it you recognised that it was not the disagreement on the subject at hand that bothered you so much, rather you were frustrated because you felt like you had not really been listened to or understood.

I think this is the crux of the matter for me also. I honestly do not have an expectation that my friends or my family could see things in the way I do or have any real concept about what it is to lose a baby and experience this grief. How could they unless they have walked that path themselves? Even then it would be different as everyone's experience (even of similar situations) can be so tremendously varied. However, what I have found upsetting and frustrating is that some of the people I hold dearest and trust with my deepest thoughts have not even given me the time or space to just express them and be listened to.

I've also considered what you said about having those needs met elsewhere. There is no doubt that I have a husband and a sister who take the time to hear me out and to listen without judgement. In a sense that need is being met elsewhere. I suppose my disappointment is the realisation that some of my friendships were not what I thought they were. For me the very essence of a good friendship is someone who makes time for another, who listens and who then acts in whatever capacity they are able to. It's not about what they can '*do*' for you, because as you have rightly pointed out, grief and pain are so extremely personal that there is probably not a lot that people can do to help carry that burden. But how are we ever to know what a friend needs or discover how we may be able to help if we never take time to ask the question? I don't think it is unreasonable to hope that our friends would listen and care for us. After all, if you can't rely upon a friend to do this for you, is it really a friendship? Isn't this the foundation of friendship?

Perhaps my reflections on friendship and expectations may also prompt you to reconsider your lack of expectations of your friends? Would you truly not be hurt if the friends you consider closest to you did not take time to listen to you or reach out to you when they knew you were going through a really rough patch? Maybe you do actually have expectations of them even though you haven't realised it. Maybe not. I'd be so glad to think that I'm not the only one making that fail this week. Good thing we're not keeping score.

I have to tell you that I love your analogy of the child injuring themselves on the concrete step. I know your intention was to illustrate a slightly different point, yet you managed to summarise in one paragraph exactly the characteristic of God it has taken me eighteen painful months to come to understand (well, a little at least). God has shown me that he is a loving, gentle father. He doesn't compromise his truth or his requirement for obedience, but he helps us through the pain and focuses us on what is important. Sometimes what is most important for me is to sit still on the couch and wait until I am feeling better, just like you said. And he is sitting there right along with me, hurting with me and waiting patiently until I am feeling better. What a tremendous friend we have in him.

Thank you for sharing your story about your friend Sarah even though it was painful for you. Embarrassingly I had to Google what BFF meant. I've seen it around so many times, and in today's vulgar society I had always assumed it meant Best F*cking Friend! But considering it was you using the term I had decided I must be mistaken. Indeed I was. Oh how I am rapidly turning into one of those embarrassing mums who does not understand what the kids are on about.

I have read previously about some of your experiences as a third culture kid, and some of the difficulties you had in assimilating back into Australian culture. It must have been hard for you as a kid to sort out your identity; even more so than the average child. You seem to have a keen insight into how you have become the person you now are. I wonder how long it has taken you to undo some of the unhealthy effects of your childhood and what has brought your transformation about? Where is it that you now find your identity?

I am going to take a stab and guess that a large part of how you view yourself is in your obsession to be a good writer. Ah, the writer's gene. I didn't realise that I had it until recently. That urge to store up every funny story, every poignant thought, every remotely interesting experience for a later date so that you can delve into the depths of the anecdotal storeroom for a written piece. I recently read a book by one of my favourite authors, Adrian Plass, in which he recounts an instance where he very nearly drowned (he can't swim) at a children's amusement park when his kids were young. It is an hilarious anecdote (in hindsight of course) yet he admits that even in the very act of nearly drowning he was simultaneously torn between the fear of imminent death and the need to make mental notes of his experience because he knew that if he survived it would make a great story. It is the best demonstration of the writer's gene I have ever come across. So, Cecily, be honest. Is it the writer's gene that is the core of your obsession or is it something else?

I too am overwhelmed by the varying and time-consuming nutritional needs of your family. I don't actually know how you have time for anything else. I am very eager to learn about your new kitchen gadget that I know absolutely nothing about. I see regular updates about the new things you have created with this utopic appliance (I think I just made up a word) and my mind boggles at a machine that can make both sorbet and stew. In my head I am envisaging an ice-cream maker has copulated with a slow-cooker, but I'm sure that can't be right. I could Google it but I'd much rather you tell me about it as I am beginning to suspect that I can't take everything that comes up on my Google search result as gospel.

I am not on the whole an unhealthy eater (although I do need to say no to more than just the occasional cupcake) yet the food I can afford for me and my family makes it incredibly difficult to lose weight and stay healthy. The most alarming discovery for me in the literature I have read is that it is entirely possible to be malnourished and overweight at the same time. So I am always thrilled to hear about your efforts in the kitchen to serve your family well.

Before I sign off, I just want to tell you not to worry about being considered bossy or a strong character. I suspect that some people view me the same way. Trite and unfresh as it sounds, God knows your heart, Cecily. As I'm sure you know, you will never be able to control what others think of you, only what comes out of you. I'm not saying that you don't have a responsibility to be sensitive to others and to adjust your approach according to the situation. Yet if you are still perceived as a bossy, strong personality, it is up to the individual to see beyond the impression and discover the gorgeous woman you are. I wish we would all take the time to get to know people better rather than judging on impressions. I'm so glad I have got to know you a little better already. You have been a blessing to me this week.

With love,

Hannah

-4-

Dear Hannah.

I have been putting off replying for several reasons. It's mostly because I've started baking all the bread our family eats because all the kids are sensitive to preservatives and a list of other stuff, and by the time I've mixed up sourdough to prove overnight *and* put all the kids to bed and read stories and snuggled so that we're connecting and enjoying each other's company *and* talked to the teenager so that I build appropriate bonds with her so that she won't go off the rails in three years time *and* said hello to my husband so that we don't get divorced in two years time because of never having communicated, the sad truth is that there's not much time left, and we both quite like our DVDs of an evening.

The other reason is that this is *hard*. Writing to you is much, much harder than I thought it was going to be. Here's the reason why: I don't actually know what I think about quite a lot of things. I can say, "x is true in my life" but then turn around and realize that really, 'y' is far more true. Or maybe it's not. And then I feel all confused and slightly dishevelled.

For example: you asked me, "Should I have expectations of my friends?" and I said, "Well, I don't. Honestly I don't." And then you said, "Really? Surely you do—at least somewhere?" and I looked in that 'somewhere' and I found some expectations. At least I think I did, but now I'm not sure whether they are real or not or whether I just made them up because I thought I ought to have expectations and with all the thinking my head is spinning a little bit.

As well as that, I keep writing for the wider audience, which is a trap, I know. I'm writing like I would write a blog post or an article, not to a specific person—ie. you, and when you write to a wider audience it's easy to slightly stretch the truth or exaggerate to make the point or just to focus solely on one topic or issue without considering the broader implications. Or I find myself constructing my words so that they make me look a certain way (serious, charming, funny or godly—take your pick according to context), which may or may not be completely true across the board.

So basically, I'm confused.

And in all of that, I'm also forgetting to say, "Hello there, how are you today?" and, "I hope your week has been better than last week because I see on Facebook that the day to day of going through life having lost two babies can be damn hard work."

Actually, I'm not very good in general at remembering to find out how other people are. It's not something that comes naturally. I have to consciously think to myself, "Greet, show interest, be kind," especially when there's a task going on as well. It's much easier to say, "Okay, let's go," than to stop and chat first. It's why I'm kind of short in my emails. I get to the point quickly and answer questions and ask them and often forget to be personal or polite. As I said in my last letter, I can get the job, whatever job it is, done. I just have to work super hard to remember the people who are involved too.

Back to the expectations. I reluctantly agree that yes, I suppose I have expectations of my friends, even though I said that I didn't so very ferociously.

My friends should, amongst other things: turn up on time, do what they say they'll do, show at least a vague interest in coming to my parties, or have a reasonable reason why they can't or won't. My friends should mostly show enjoyment in my company; they should be fairly good listeners or make a reasonable fist at pretending to listen. I expect a moderate balance of turn-taking in conversation, depending on the circumstances. If there was a death in the immediate family, I'd expect a card at a minimum and a phone call or two over the next couple of months. I'd also expect that where they were able, they could help me out if I asked for something that wasn't over the top.

I think what I'm saying is that I expect politeness and reliability. As well as affection, and occasionally, going an extra mile or three. If people can't give me those basics, I don't call them 'friends'. They might be nice acquaintances or people I like to talk to on the playground at school but I don't put them in the proper friend category.

But maybe you're talking about a different category of 'friend'. You talked about the people who really knew your heart and who you were very, very close to. I'm not sure, but I think I don't have many of those. And if I *do* have them, I'm just so grateful that they think I'm nice that I can't even start to put added expectations on them.

I think I'm of the opinion that expectations can kill a close friendship. It happened to me a few years out of uni. I had met this girl, Anne, while we were both studying law, and, as occasionally happens, we both clicked from day one. We got married around the same time and our husbands enjoyed each others' company as well so we started to hang out together. Anne would often say, "You're my best friend, Cec, you're such a good friend." She said it at length and with such passion that it almost made me uncomfortable, but I loved the way she made me feel very special. I figured she was a bit gushy but that was okay. She was a great friend to me and I really loved spending time with her. It's just that it started to become incredibly hard to pin her down. We'd arrange to meet for lunch in the city but three out of four times she'd ring at the last minute. "I can't come, I'm too busy! I'm so sorry!" It got so I'd make an arrangement but I'd know that it wouldn't happen. This went on for two or three years. I was frustrated. I felt that she should give me more. That if she said I was her best friend, she should show it. That she put everything else, especially her work, ahead of me as a priority.

It came to a head one day for me when she'd arranged to meet me somewhere at 1pm. At this stage I had a baby. Being a first time mother, I was a bit fussy about times and naps (these days I wouldn't care) and I'd said 1pm because it seemed to tie in with feeding. Anne didn't turn up until 2pm, which, as you know, can knock a new mother's routine right out of the water. When she finally tapped on the door with an excuse that I didn't feel was good enough I was absolutely furious with her. "Why do you always do this? It's not good enough. Rah rah rah." I picked a fight and she fought back and we argued for about half an hour. At the end we left on what appeared to be goodish terms, but let me tell you, the friendship was never the same. After another 12 months it petered out completely and I haven't seen her or been in contact for over ten years.

She didn't fulfill my expectations. But then, I realize that I may not have fulfilled hers either. Anne was a talented 'gift-giver'. (I'm sure you've read about the five 'love languages' so you'll know what I'm talking about.) She once walked the length of the Rocks Markets with the flu looking for the perfect pair of earrings for me. And she was right. I absolutely loved those earrings. Unfortunately I'm not so committed to gifts and once I gave her something that, while it was lovely, was a re-gift. Unfortunately for me she found out! Perhaps that was where it all started to go downhill for her.

With ten years of hindsight and a little bit more maturity, I can see that Anne was never, ever going to fulfil my expectations. She was always going to run late, flip priorities and focus on the 'what's urgent that's going on now' rather than on the 'what's coming up on the schedule'. That's what made her so vivacious and interesting. I, on the other hand, was never, ever going to be able to give her hand-chosen gifts that met her need for beauty, art and passion. I'm just not that person. But I am reliable and on time and steady and good at doing the dishes.

I think we could have continued our friendship but with the understanding that we couldn't meet each other's expectations. It wouldn't have been as intense, perhaps, but maybe it would have been more freeing?

I think about being married and how I have certain expectations of my husband and he has certain expectations of me. (Mine are mostly about washing up properly and putting dirty socks in the laundry, by the way.) I would estimate that on average we've had ten big conversations per year about our expectations of each other. We've been married nearly 18 years, so you can do the maths. Some of those conversations have been easy. Lots have been uncomfortable. Some have been absolutely torturous. The only reason we are able to keep going with each through the difficult adjustments is because we're committed to each other. A verbal commitment to 'honour and cherish' and all the rest of it stands for a lot. But with friends, for the most part, there is no verbal commitment. (Maybe if you've been best friends since the age of six you might have sworn loyalty or even cut your fingers and mixed the blood or something...) But most adult friendships don't have a verbal commitment which makes it very awkward to approach talking about any difficulties.

Perhaps expectations come from the idea of wanting to get back what you give. That would make sense with what I experienced with Anne. I 'gave' time, organization and reliability to her. I expected to get the same back. She 'gave' me great presents, which mine weren't even close to matching. Neither of us got back what we put into the relationship. And of course, the theory of the love languages is that we all have preferred love languages. We tend to speak our own though, and we tend to not hear anyone else's.

I'm sorry you've got to be thinking about all of this at the same time as dealing with grief and sorrow and all the rest. Unfortunately I think that's how it goes though. When life is normal, stuff goes unnoticed. It's when it's hard and you have no margins or reserves or resources to spare that things that have been niggles before become suddenly too uncomfortable to live with.

After my son was diagnosed with autism I got depression and was sent off to see a counsellor to get some help. I wanted to talk about my feelings about the autism, but she was more interested in other stuff in my life: boarding school, family, Pakistan, my attitude towards myself. Actually, that's happened every time I've ever been to see a counsellor—and there have been a few. I go in wanting to talk about, for example, my phobia of hearing people breathe (yes, it's true), and they want to talk about attachment issues.

Which is annoying.

But I suppose it's a bit like cleaning my house (which I don't do that often or that well). It would be far better to have a system and some organization and a place for everything before I start cleaning than to just sweep and tidy and then become confounded because there's nowhere to get rid of the debris. Or, let's take cooking, another task that I've never enjoyed or been good at. Now that I've had to think more about it, with all the food intolerances, and really go to the core of what I'm doing, things are actually becoming easier. Who would have guessed that having a meal plan and a shopping list could help so much? In other words, you've got to get stuff sorted out so you've got room to deal with other stuff that pops up.

Actually, I've always been a person who likes to go to the core of an issue. My mum often says, about some grand pronouncement that I've made, "Oh, that's too deep for me," but I love to analyse what's *really* going on underneath in any given situation. My husband is fairly similar to me and often our arguments will turn from an argument about, for example, socks being left on the floor, to an argument about the way we are actually arguing. We often talk about the 'process' being more important than the 'content'. Some people like parties and dancing and going out, but I get my kicks from having an analytical, in-depth conversation about what's at the heart of, say, my dislike of the colour red (and yes, that's also true).

I'm done with this topic. My head is spinning. I'll move on to something much easier: the writer's gene, although that phrase doesn't sit very well with me. I'm not sure why. Is it a gene? Or a passion? If, like a gene, it's inherited, why do I have it but none of my family do? But if it's a passion, how is it kindled? And how come some people find it easy and others can't write to save themselves?

All I know is that I've wanted to be a writer since the day, at the age of eight, I heard my name called out as the winner of the White Essay Cup at the British Overseas School in Karachi, Pakistan. I was sitting about three quarters of the way down the lines, on the right and when they said, "Cecily" my legs went wobbly and I could hardly breathe. I was only in Year Three and I had beaten every other primary aged child in the school by writing a story in which I went back in time through eating a chocolate frog. They gave me a trophy as big as my head and, if it still exists, it has my name on it twice, for 1981 and 1983.

In 1982, when our family was back in Australia for six months (and I missed my opportunity to win three in a row) I walked past an Angus and Robertson bookshop at Miranda

Fair. In the window was a display by a popular writer. I don't even know who it was. But in that second I knew that my aim was to fill a window with books written by me. It has been a driving force of my life for a very long time.

And yes, I know what Adrian Plass was talking about when he thought, 'this near death experience could be good for a book.' I am forever observing my own feelings and emotions and mentally storing things away for future use. I can almost dissociate from myself—especially in times of heavy emotion—leave my body and watch myself. But it's not only for stories. I watch out for things for my blog too. In fact, to my shame, my first thought on hearing your talk at Esther's funeral was, 'This should be published. People should read this.' I had to stop myself rushing up to you to ask if you would mind. Not exactly the most sensitive thing to say to grieving parents.

And here's my question for you: what do you *do* when you feel sad? I wrote something on grief for a young adult a few weeks ago with some ideas on 'how to grieve' but I'm thinking everything sounded just too organized. Life is a lot more messy and annoying. How do you manage?

Cecily x

-5-

Dear Cecily,

I have tried to write a reply to your letter a few times now, and I just can't. I am consumed with sadness.

I miss my babies.

I will write to you as soon as I am able.

With love,

Hannah

-6-

Dear Hannah,

Words and big long letters and theories and everything are a bit pointless right now.

I'd give you a hug—multiple hugs—if I were near you.

Then I'd probably make you dinner, vacuum your house and put some (calorie-free obviously) chocolate cake in your fridge. Then I'd tuck you up in bed, let you have a cry and a sleep and then take you out for a walk around the lake with the autumn leaves coming down and try some lame jokes to make you laugh.

After that I'd go home and feel sad myself and then pray for you a couple of times a day.

I've got nothing else. Except to say I wish it wasn't so. I wish it hadn't happened. I wish you didn't feel so bad.

I'm Sad and I Need Cake

This world is a very hard place to live in sometimes.

Love, Cecily

-7-

Hi Cec,

Sorry it's taken me so long to reply. Thank-you for your last letter especially; I bawled when I read it. I must admit that the calorie-free chocolate cake part was the most exciting for me, but I loved it all. It was like reading a warm hug. Thank you.

I'm sitting here struggling to know where to start. Now I'm the one who has been putting off writing the letter. Admittedly, it has mostly been because I have been such an emotional wreck these past weeks that trying to do anything other than get dressed, look after my family and cry my eyes out for a good portion of the day is simply not possible. Yesterday when I mentally allocated time to reply to your letter today I felt like I could do it, but as I come to write today

I'm feeling quite flat. So I apologise if this is not very dynamic or doesn't even really follow on very well from your last.

By the way, thanks for your long letter. It came on a day when I really needed it. I had had an extremely tough week. I was coming off almost two months of slowing down and being selfish with my time to process my own emotions and grief, to being thrust into a week that was chock-full of having to give oodles of my time towards other people and their needs, which is totally fine in principle but a real shock to the system in reality, especially for a staunch introvert. I woke up on the morning I received your letter quite teary and snappy with my family (probably not helped along by the fact that Michael and I were up numerous times during the night with two children who were having issues sleeping).

I loved reading your letter. I laughed and I cried, quite literally actually (which was a bit embarrassing seeing as I was reading it at my local coffee shop). I am slightly ashamed to admit however that when I finished reading it (and this will expose the shallow nature of my character) I thought to myself, *Yes, but what about the Thermomix™? She didn't mention the Thermomix™!* So I still find myself wondering about your new kitchen gadget.

To tie up the friendship and expectations thread for now, I'll end by filling you in on what has happened with my friendships situation. I think that between the two of us we have (as we both love to do) examined the underlying issues fairly thoroughly.

Prior to receiving your letter I had already come to realise that some of my friends were just not going to be able to give me what I needed; perhaps with fair or poor reason on their part—it is not for me to judge. But I had realised that my love and appreciation for them was as strong as it ever was, so I didn't want to go down the path of confrontation and risk breaking the friendships altogether. I am blessed to know these wonderful people, and a little of them in my life is better than none at all. And I am very happy with this decision.

Incidentally, I haven't read the *Five Love Languages* book (it has been on my to-read list for a long time) but I understand the basic principle behind it. I actually realised a long time ago that these particular friends do speak quite different love languages to my own, and although it did niggle at me occasionally I was generally okay with it. But as you astutely pointed out in your letter, it is often the times of stress and hardship that can make those niggles unbearable.

I thought about this sort of strain a lot after I lost Stephen, as some of my family relationships and friendships (some of the same friendships by the way) began to fall apart. The little niggles became big issues. Most prominently I remember days and weeks where it was almost unbearable to be around my children. Love them dearly? Yes! I did. But they were (at the time) two and a half and three and a half years old, and both of them were in that delightful never-ending-questions phase. You know the one– you give one answer to a question and the immediate response is, "but why?"

It was torturous. I believe that my children deserve to have good and accurate answers to their questions, and I tried so hard to be patient with them. Yet my mind was so consumed with grief that I could hardly think straight about what I was going to wear or what I was going to cook for dinner that I found the constant barrage of questions very hard to take. I desperately wanted to be patient with them, but I failed miserably. Many times I snapped and lost it because I just could not take the questions. Often I found myself frozen in thought because I couldn't even process what they had asked in order to give them an answer. It wasn't that they were being naughty or unkind. It was because my resistance was down, causing something that normally took a fair amount of patience to bear to become excruciating.

I've been thinking of an analogy to help explain what it is like to people who have never been put under severe emotional stress, and all I can come up with is an illustration of a balloon. Imagine you had a latex balloon covered with tiny slits. If you were to fill the balloon with a small amount of water that only stretched the balloon a little, perhaps some of the slits may leak a bit, but generally the water will stay in the balloon. It's not until there is pressure in the balloon as it is being filled with more and more water that the slits become stretched and more apparent, for by that stage water is leaking everywhere. The more water forced into the balloon, the greater the intensity of the leak as it spurts forth. So it is with the niggles in our lives. We can know they are there and occasionally a drop of frustration may leak out, but most of the time we can keep it together. But when we are filled with intense emotions and stress we are stretched beyond our ability to keep it all in and water starts pissing all over the place.

Sorry for the use of the vulgar term, but I use it because it is precisely how I have felt in recent weeks. Pissed off. Piss everywhere. And I hate it. At times I was getting immensely frustrated with people and situations so easily that I took to staying at home and not talking to anyone or even sending emails. I couldn't deal with it. I once read on a grief support website that people who are grieving are more accident prone because their minds and emotions are so preoccupied with their grief that they are not able to physically function at the same level. I suppose it's like getting 2GB of RAM to do 3GB of processing—it can't happen. Something's got to give. This is my life at the moment. I can't even make simple decisions. I can't think about future plans. The other day someone asked me for my surname and I drew a blank. It took me a full ten seconds to remember what my surname was. I hate it. I feel debilitated. I am usually a multi-tasker extraordinaire.

Thankfully, the last day or so has not been filled with as much anger. Unfortunately though, it has been filled with more sadness. But I guess it has to be filled with something, right? Now I lock myself away at home because I am struggling to keep a lid on my sorrow, and I hate the thought of being a bubbling mess in front of anyone else.

It's not because of pride—at least I don't think it is. It's because I think that in talking to someone else about what I am going through I will have to bring them up to speed to where I am at (which I can't articulate half of the time because I don't even know within myself), and I think that the whole process will add more pain on top of what I am already feeling.

I hope there will come a time when I can talk to other people face to face about how I am because I know how much it helped me to do that after Stephen died. But I think that time may be a fair way in the future. And, once again, I realise I have more expectations upon my friends; to bear with me through all of this. I am frightened that they will be put off by my apparent lack of interest in their lives or my constant refusal to "get together" with them.

The irony is that a month or so ago, all I wanted to do was talk and spend time with people and not many opportunities were forthcoming. Now people are almost banging down my door wanting to talk and see how I'm doing, and I don't feel I can. It will be a wonder if I come through this process with any friends at all, and if I do it will be testimony to them, and not to me.

So this leads me to answer the lingering question from your last letter; what do I do when I am sad? Apparently I don't do very well at all. Honestly, part of me resents the fact that I am fast becoming something of an authority on the subject. And yes, before you mention it, there are some God-issues I am working through here at the moment. It's not the "why me, God?" or the "how could you, God?" issues that I feel people assume I have; but it's something. I'm just not sure what it is yet.

At the risk of sounding like a counselor, I think I have learned to let myself "just be." To take each day as it comes. If I'm angry, then I'm angry. If I'm devastated, then I'm devastated. If I find myself having a happy moment, or even several, then it's okay to enjoy those too. I think the trick is to surround yourself with people who can let you be all of these things, and to allow yourself to be what you need to without being unfair to those people.

For example, if you are angry as part of a deep grief process you are likely to have outbursts of anger with the people immediately in your range, even though you probably aren't angry with them. Under normal circumstances I would be a huge advocate for controlling the anger and not misdirecting it (even though admittedly I fail at this all too often). However, for someone who is grieving, sometimes they just need to be allowed to be angry. I'm not condoning hurtful remarks, actions, abuse or carelessness—there is a level of restraint that needs to be exercised. But for someone who is deeply grieving, they are probably already using up whatever energy they already have in trying to control their emotions on a moment to moment basis, so the ability to control powerful emotions is severely diminished.

Being allowed to go through a range of emotions can help the grief process along. I know I sometimes don't even know why I feel angry until I've seen and heard myself being angry. Recently, I've come to realise that although the emotion presents itself as anger, it isn't anger at all. It is deep, deep sadness. I probably wouldn't have understood that if my husband and children hadn't been patient with me and given me the space just to feel what I was feeling. I've also had to apologise and ask forgiveness for outbursts that have been directed towards them unfairly. I love my family so much, and I can't imagine what it is like for people to grieve when they don't have the space in their home and their immediate family to process how they need to process.

So, that's the emotional side of things. But what to do while all this is whizzing around inside? I don't just sit and stare at the wall. Actually, I probably go overboard with activity. I get busy. Anything to keep my hands occupied; something that requires some sort of concentration, but nothing too complex as my brain is working on other things. For me, it's craft stuff. I come from a family of crafties. In fact when Michael first met me and was describing me to his friends who hadn't yet met me, he kept using the term 'crafty'. I was not overly enamoured with this description.

Nevertheless, I suppose you could say I am crafty. I quite like hand-sewing because I can do it whilst sitting in a comfy chair, watching TV, waiting for kids to finish ballet lessons, waiting at the doctor's rooms etc. I took up cross stitch when Stephen was diagnosed with his condition because I knew I would have a lot of time sitting around waiting in hospitals and doctors' surgeries. It also helped to distract me from what was going on.

About three weeks ago, in a desperate bid to find something new to keep my hands and mind occupied, I learned how to crochet. YouTube is wonderful. I can sit in my study at 11pm when everyone else is in bed and receive private tutorials. Crochet is now my new thing. In the space of three weeks I have crocheted one adult beanie, three children's beanies and two large scarves. I have crocheted my fingers down to stumps.

I suppose this is an important part of being sad too. Being able to put life on hold for a while. Of course there are some things that you just can't shut down. But put as much off as you can until you are feeling better. I have cancelled most of my activities outside of the house until further notice. I'm not playing piano at church at the moment. I also gave away being a leader at my local play group. I've postponed running our bible study group. I've deferred my counseling studies until next semester. I'm not even going to every engagement like I normally would—birthdays, girls days, prayer days etc. I haven't volunteered for canteen duty or uniform shop duty at the new school. Not yet. I'm just enjoying time at home to do all of the things I have told you about. I know I can't stay at home and crochet forever, and I know that I won't. I will pick up these other activities if and when I am ready, and as God leads me. Sometimes I think God uses these down times in life to give us space to examine and pray about the things we are involved with and to consider whether or not it's still what we need to be doing. Some things are and some things need to be let go.

On a slightly different note, I was pleased to read your analogy about tidying your home. I so agree with what you said. Furthermore, I am a big believer that 95 per cent of the time a person's home is a reflection of themselves and consequently their lives. For example, I have a home with quite big open spaces that I enjoy welcoming people into. There is a lot of light and openness about our house, and I have done my best to furnish it elegantly within our means and to keep it tidy. However, there are some rooms and cupboards in my house that I would never let anyone other than myself or my husband go. My bedroom for example, is right by the front door. Both Michael and I work at keeping the bedroom tidy; bed made and clothes off the floor, so that most of the time we are happy to leave the door open when people visit our home.

Then there are the other rooms. I call them the dump-and-run rooms. These are the rooms where I dump things that I don't have time to deal with at that moment. From time to time I chip away at the edges in an attempt to get things back into order or find a lost item. Then maybe once every twelve months I sift through it all, sort and tidy, and everything is okay for a while. Until I let it happen all over again. The rubbish piles up fast. Real fast.

So too it is with my life. I try to make an effort to be a welcoming and inviting person—to be open and honest.

What you see is what you get. Like my bedroom, there are some aspects of my life that are private just because they are private. People might get a glimpse of these things from the outside as they walk past, but it's really nothing for them to be involved with. Then there are the messy parts of my life; the areas that I don't like anyone else to even catch a glimpse of so I keep them out. For me, these spaces are usually cluttered up with the sins of pride and selfishness (among others), and it seems like I am forever trying to sort them out. It's a constant battle. Then every so often I win the battle, things get sorted, and quick as a flash it starts piling up again.

There is one room in particular in my home that up until yesterday has been out of bounds to everyone, including myself. It is a room that, unfortunately, is situated at the centre of our home; anyone who comes into the main area will notice whether or not the door to this room is open or closed. It sits right next to the kitchen and family area where the hub of family life takes place—just off to the side.

This was the room set aside first for Stephen, and then for Esther. I cannot explain to you the depth of my sorrow when I consider that twice now—two separate times—I have not been able to bring home the precious little baby for whom this room has been so lovingly prepared. I have hardly been able to set foot into it since I came home from the hospital with empty arms earlier this year.

Like many other rooms in my house it started off as a dump-and-run room. Every blanket, bear and memento given to us for Esther was stashed in there to be dealt with later. As the months have passed it has become a no-go zone. About a month ago I had to go in there once when I was doing a late-night tidy up after everyone else had gone to bed. It was almost midnight and I opened the door to place the item inside. As I swung open the door I could just make out the shape of the cot and the change table from the hallway light, and for the tiniest moment I felt like I had gone into my baby's room in the middle of the night to comfort her or to feed her, just as every mother does after they have a baby. But the reality of the situation broke sharply through, sending a chill down my body, and I promptly turned and fled.

I think this sums up my current state perfectly. My grief is always with me; it stares at me relentlessly, whatever I am doing—just a little off to the side. I can distract myself for a time and not think about it, but it is still there. I can even leave the house and be far away from it for a time, but it is always there when I come back. And everyone that comes into my life at the moment can see it, plain as day. They can also sense that the door is firmly shut.

I have been trying so hard to keep the door closed. I think the sadness that would flood through the door would consume and overwhelm me if I dared to open it. It would wipe me out so I couldn't be there for my family. It would drown me so that I couldn't function. It would put people off because I would be soaking wet.

No dry person wants to hug a wet person.

Interestingly though, yesterday I had to do something about it. I needed to sort out Esther's room because we have to change the sleeping arrangements for our other children sooner rather than later. I knew that I was not ready to change it into a room for one of my other children straight away. Not yet. Another little dark, no-go area in my life has been the section of my walk-in-robe housing the wall decals I had purchased to finish off Esther's room. While I was waiting for the fresh wall paint to cure so I could put them up, Esther died.

Before I could even contemplate turning the room into something else, I knew I had to finish what I had started. I had been immensely eager to finish her room before she was born, so I guess I shouldn't have been surprised to find it was still incredibly important to me to finish it now. But I was.

Cecily, yesterday was truly one of the hardest days of my life, decorating and primping a nursery for a baby who will never get to use it, again. I cried all day. I was exhausted. But when it was finished I was also thrilled. I never thought it was something that I needed to do. It was so impractical, and

I am a pragmatist through and through. But it is beautiful. And sad. But mostly beautiful.

What's more, the door to that room has been left open all night and all day today. I've actually enjoyed peering in each time I've walked past. The kids were even playing in there this morning and it didn't bother me at all (especially as they packed up afterwards, even though it was on pain of death.)

So I think it's a good start. Emotionally, that door is still shut, but if my theory of houses is anything to go by then perhaps it's not too long before I can pry open the door a little.

How about you, Cecily? Care to share some things about the rooms in your house? And don't forget the kitchen. .. there is a gadget in your kitchen that I would especially like to hear about.

With love,

Hannah

-8-

Dear Hannah,

You will have noticed that there has been no letter from me over the school holidays. This is because when I haven't been stuck in the kitchen (yes, using my Thermomix™) I have been answering endless questions, refereeing endless fighting and sewing endless world flags into a quilt for my seven year-old.

I don't do holidays well. Like you, I am an introvert I and I desperately need my quiet time. I also thrive on achievement—but it has to be the kind of achievement that doesn't just get eaten up 20 minutes after it has been cooked.

In addition, these holidays my son with autism had a particularly difficult withdrawal reaction from the goat's cheese he has been eating for the last couple of months. I gave it to him a while ago hoping that it wouldn't be a problem like cow's milk cheese is for him, but his diet ended up being so limited by the end that his doctor suggested he gave the cheese a miss for a while and from the strength of the withdrawal, I think we can safely say that we have done the right thing.

For an entire week my son dedicated his existence to annihilating his brother. He insulted him, belittled him, annoyed him, refused to be in the same room as him, refused to leave when I asked him to and pretty much whinged about everything that went on around him.

I tried lots of things: getting cross with him, separating them, threatening no TV and ignoring it. Nothing worked. The only thing that had the slightest impact on the situation was to completely ignore the troublemaker and to hug and kiss the victim.

I consider myself quite a competent person but nothing has thrown me for six more than attempting to effectively parent a child with autistic spectrum disorder. I am frequently at a loss, at the end of my abilities and with no more ideas. I need help from professionals! That's kind of embarrassing.

His issues have a ripple effect into the rest of the family as well. When he went to stay with his grandparents for three nights I saw his little brother visibly relax and blossom. He talked more, he enjoyed life more and he seemed less stressed. I was less stressed too. And because of that we all seemed to have more fun. In fact while he was away I noticed just how much stress autism still adds to our family, even though I had thought that we were mostly okay now. At the beginning, life was chaos and a walking disaster, but things are so much better now that I imagined we were fairly close to normal. It's once the stress is taken off for a while that you realise how much is still there day-to-day.

Living with autism has meant that I parent the others differently too. For example, my kids don't really have jobs around the house. They have a small amount of responsibility for making sure their rooms are reasonably tidy, but I am not strict about it. They get themselves dressed and pack their own bags but they don't wash up or clean up or sort the washing or sweep the floor or take regular responsibility for anything that isn't theirs alone. At dinner time I ask them to set the table for me but the amount of grumbling that goes on from the child with ASD is almost too painful to bear— every single night.

I didn't expect it would be like this, believe me. By this age I wanted them to be more involved in the family jobs, but Cameron just really can't cope at this stage and it seems completely unfair to let him off but make the others do it. So

I live constantly with the slight anxiety that I am doing it wrong and that my children will lack the skills they need to be competent adults.

In any case, the holidays are over now and I can relax and recover from what feels like a two-week assault on my emotions.

I can also cook in peace. This is the point in the letter where your questions about my Thermomix™ will be answered. I had started another letter with a list of the things that my Thermo can do but it seemed boring and rather like a brochure so instead I will tell you about my afternoon of cooking.

Just to be clear, I am cooking all dairy-free, soy-free and preservative-free because of my children's food intolerances. I am also cooking some gluten-free because the gluten-free/casein-free (GF-CF) diet suits my son with autism very well. There is also a list of about twelve other different things they are intolerant of, including malt, brewer's yeast, peas, mushrooms and bananas.

Basically, they can eat almost nothing out of packets.

The effects are on behaviour, cognition and gut function. All of them have compacted bowels and poor nutrient absorption and they are all picky eaters. I could write a whole other essay about my trials with food and my children's eating habits.

Anyway, to the cooking.

There was nothing to eat for snacks so I decided to make no bake chocolate cookies and some brownies. I used the Thermo to melt the coconut oil and the chocolate for five minutes. Then I added quinoa flakes and mixed the batter for four seconds before spreading it in a pan and popping in the fridge. The total time for this was about six minutes. For the brownies, I added all the ingredients together before whizzing them on speed 4 for eight seconds and then spread them into a pan and baked it all in the oven. Total time, including washing up the Thermomix™ bowl, and re-dressing the naked toddler in the middle of it all was about four minutes.

After that I whipped up a buckwheat crêpe batter in one and a half minutes, which included tipping the batter out into a bowl and washing up the Thermo. (Cooking the crêpes on the flat grill sandwich maker took a lot longer, but I did it in between the rest of the afternoon's work.) The crêpes served as the lasagne noodles for the gluten-free/dairy free lasagne I made next.

I didn't make the meat sauce in the Thermo, although I could have. I did, however, use it to grind the onion, garlic, carrot and zucchini (yes, I am the Queen of hidden vegetables) before cooking the sauce on the stove top. I have done a Bolognese sauce before from start to finish in 20 minutes in the Thermo and it was delicious. This time, however, I needed it for the white sauce, which is ready with no stirring or mucking around in 12 minutes.

Of course, nothing ever goes as smoothly as you'd like, right? I had decided to make the dairy-free white sauce based on rice milk and we had no more rice milk in the fridge, so I had to make some. I whizzed up brown rice, a few cashews and sunflower seeds and a calcium tablet into a fine flour. That took about a minute. Then I added water and cooked it for about six minutes at 80°. After that I whizzed it up again before straining it into a jug. Voila, rice milk.

After that it was a simple case of adding the ingredients for the white sauce, setting the time and the temperature and leaving it alone so I could focus on the crêpes.

After that I realised that the kids didn't have any ice cream in the freezer. So I grabbed a can and a half of coconut milk, poured it into the Thermo with sugar and two eggs, set the time and the speed and temperature, and walked away. Eight minutes later I had a perfect creme anglaise ready to go into the ice cream maker.

That was my afternoon's work. Later that night I spent six minutes putting on and kneading two batches of bread dough which was used for sandwiches the next day.

I haven't mentioned the spinach smoothie I made for breakfast or the raspberry sorbet I whipped up for my Bible study a few weeks ago. I also haven't mentioned the fact that it makes the best risotto I've ever tasted, all with no stirring or hassle. I've also been whizzing up ground chicken to hide in plain rice and sauces so that the kids will actually eat protein without knowing it.

It's a lifesaver. An expensive lifesaver, I grant you. At $2,000 or thereabouts you need to consider whether it's worth it but for me it makes every day liveable instead of a huge burden.

Because I am not a cook. I've never enjoyed cooking. To me, cooking is something you have to do so that you can get on with your day and do the really fun things in life. So to now be in a position where I need to cook everything that goes into my children's mouths feels like a bit of a prison sentence, where the kitchen is my cell and the exercise yard is walking back and forth to the pantry. The Thermomix™ is my parole papers. My ticket to a future outside of food.

How were your school holidays? Were you able to cope with your children the way you hoped to? Are you still crocheting or have you moved on? And are you still looking into Esther's room and enjoying it? I was so delighted to read that you had finished decorating it and were happy with it.

The pictures of the finished product were beautiful. You have very good taste.

I could comment on many parts of your last letter, but I especially liked what you said about dry people not wanting to hug wet people.

I was talking to a friend over the holidays (we met up at Maccas for a playdate) who told me about the time she went out for a work dinner and ended up sitting next to the wife of one of her co-workers, whom she'd never met. The woman had a son who had multiple, serious allergies to everything. I mean, I thought my kids were bad—this woman's reality was a disaster. Anyway, all night, my friend heard about this woman's issues. She had nothing else to talk about. It was all food and environment and safety and the trouble with schools and public places and the evils of air fresheners and the daily struggles she had to deal with.

My friend said, "It was interesting. I mean, really it was. But she had nothing else to talk about and I ended up feeling battered. Like I never wanted to talk to her again."

You know, I felt so sorry for them both. I felt sorry for my friend, because she was the dry person that day. She wanted to hug, at least for a short time, but she was getting wetter and wetter. And I felt sorry for the woman with the son with the serious problems because I know how it feels to only be able to talk about the overwhelming issues you're facing. They're so big and you're so alone in it all, and you're so worried and you feel like you're not doing enough and you're a failure as a parent and you're angry with the rest of the world because it seems like no-one cares or wants to help and no-one can fix the problem. This woman was wet but she was pulling my friend back into the pool with her.

I came home and thought, "I need to write something about grief and worry and how to manage it socially so that everyone else doesn't get overwhelmed and then start to avoid you." Because that's what can happen so often. I know I've avoided the person with the chronic, unsolvable problems that they can't stop talking about. But then I've also been the person with the chronic, unsolvable problems that I have to fight to keep from falling out of my mouth. Somehow, someone needs to carry a towel so that the wetness is caught and the hug can happen but in a way that everyone can cope with.

I was emailing another friend over the holidays who had written an article about grief that she wanted to run past me. She's had a lot of hard times and many losses and in some ways she's been broken permanently by it all.

She wrote that part of what she was dealing with was the shame of not being able to be resilient 'enough'. As a Christian, you're 'supposed' to be able to deal with whatever gets thrown your way, but she felt that loss upon loss upon loss had made her *less* resilient. That old adage, 'What doesn't kill you makes you stronger,' hasn't been proved true for her. She feels she's been slowly whittled down to a half-death kind of existence where the tears leak out holes that never seem to heal.

I wonder if sometimes we are impatient with the broken people because we think they 'ought' to be better by now, as if we get to set the time that's allowable for grief and recovery. We have so much intolerance for other people's pain, both as individuals and as church. In her article my friend said that people who had pat answers hadn't suffered enough yet. I think that may be true.

By the way, much to my disappointment, there's probably no such thing as calorie free chocolate cake. Not even the Thermomix™ is that good.

Cecily xx

-9-

Dear Cecily,

Well, school has been back for two weeks now, so I am wondering how you are getting on. I felt physically drained when I read the first part of your last letter. School holidays sounded like a marathon effort for you. Having just survived my first ever school holidays since Allison started school this year, I had already begun to suspect that the purpose of the school term is to give parents a chance to recover in between school holidays. Now that I've read your letter I am certain of it.

I hardly know what I could say to you to give you some sort of encouragement about the way you are raising your children, and in particular Cameron. Because I have not had to face the sort of stress and complexities of trying to parent a child with autism I feel ill-equipped to offer any sort of meaningful support. I am extremely conscious that whatever I say may be well meant and kindly received, but probably not a great deal more because I can only imagine what you are going through, and even then I'm sure my imagination fails me. But I desperately want to try and give you some sort of encouragement, so I shall attempt it and ask for your forgiveness if I am totally unhelpful.

I hear you say in your letter that you feel wholly at the end of your abilities and out of ideas. I think most parents can relate to this one way or another, even if they don't have children with autism. Children frequently push us to our limits and put us in situations we never dreamed we would be in. I know that I never envisaged wearing my husband's industrial grade ear muffs around the house to block out the sound of a crying baby for just 20 minutes so I didn't go insane. True story.

I also hear your concern about your other children; wondering if and how they will learn what they need to learn in order to become competent adults, and be able to look after themselves and families of their own, and I offer the following thoughts in the hope that it may ease your mind slightly.

First of all, don't worry about them not knowing how to use a steam mop or operate the washing machine, or undertake other chores which you have very wisely decided not to divvy up amongst the kids. When my husband and I first started living together he didn't even know what a toilet brush was used for. Trust me, they learn quick. And let's face it, by the time they move out of home technology will have moved on so that floors will probably be cleaned by some infra-red device and clothes will be dirt resistant (I hope), so the current way of doing things may very well be obsolete.

Secondly, I have been thinking about the strength of character that is being built in your children as they learn to live with a difficult person, and also as they watch you and your hubby love him and instruct him. To explain what I mean I offer an example from my own life.

I have copped a lot of flack from doctors and nurses about not protecting my children more from the trauma of losing a brother and then a sister. By their definition, 'protecting them' would include not telling them ahead of time that Stephen was very sick and likely not to live for very long, not including Stephen as part of the family whilst he was still inside my belly, not allowing the children to meet and hold Esther after she was born, and not to have a professional photographer come and take family photos during the few precious hours we were all together, to name only a few. I shall never forget the horrified look on the midwife's face when I announced I had asked my parents to bring Allison and Harry to the hospital so they could meet their baby sister and have photos together.

And I won't lie to you, Cec, it was hard. Very hard. Even now I find it hard to look at the photos of Allison holding Esther and seeing her grief-stricken face. But then I look at the photos of Harry; devastated by his loss but also visibly chuffed to be finally holding the baby sister he had been looking forward to meeting for so long. In both cases I am so glad that I did not deny my children the opportunity to meet their baby sister, hard though it was, and I am absolutely certain that as adults they will treasure the memory and the photos even more.

In the meantime however, I face the complexities and questions of two children who have lost two baby siblings. Every time there is an infant baptism or dedication at church Harry wants to know if it is happening because the baby is going to die. Allison keeps telling me that she doesn't want to get married and have children because she doesn't want her babies to die. So I say it again, it is hard. Very hard.

But do you know what the enormous blessing is in all of this? I have seen my children offer comfort, empathy and love to people who are hurting in a way that many adults are inept at doing, let alone children of their age. Their hurt and devastating experiences have built a strength of character in them that could not have come from any other experience, and I am absolutely certain that God will use this to grow them and to serve others, for which I am delighted.

So too can I see opportunities for your children to build virtues of patience, grace, tolerance, understanding and empathy, and they are only the ones I can think of. Is it hard? Absolutely. But the things you and Andrew are teaching all of your children by shepherding them in the way you are will build character in them that will help them to cope with whatever situation they find themselves in. It might not be the competent, keep-it-together, neat and tidy parenting you had always envisaged, but trust me, even if you were fulfilling that dream you'd be neglecting something or making mistakes. No person or situation is perfect after all. And you and I both have the blessing of knowing that whatever shortfalls come in our parenting (and I know there are many in mine) that God himself works in and around our efforts, and builds knowledge and character within our children in a way that is impossible for us to do. After a day of parenting fails this is the only thought that gives me relief enough to sleep.

Okay, so now it's my turn to be feeling insecure about what I've written. The only thing that stops me from deleting everything I've written so far is that you were honest enough to tell me in your very first letter that you were unsure about what you had said, so it would hardly be fair for me to chicken out.

To be honest, it is how I am feeling a lot at the moment; young, vulnerable, and unsure about everything. After you mentioned it in your last letter, I read your article on grief as well as a few others, and I'm feeling incredibly stupid. I would like to have thought that I had some amazing insight into grieving seeing as I've done so much of it, but it seems as though every other writer who has taken the time to jot down some thoughts about grief has more insight on the topic than I have.

For example, in my last letter I tried to respond to you about what I do when I feel sad. I cringe to think about what I wrote and I can't even bring myself to go back and read it because I am sure now that it was the biggest load of rubbish I've ever written. I have some vague memory of trying to tie it together all very nicely as a written analogy of a messy house where I conveniently left a little door open for my grief to start to peek through so I can start processing. Bollocks. Let me tell you what happened within about two days of writing that last letter.

Two words: panic attacks. Truly some of the most terrifying experiences of my life. That little door to my grief that I had mentally pulled ajar after decorating Esther's room was blown off its hinges and caught me totally by surprise.

It's one of the reasons I feel so stupid. All this time I have honestly felt like I have been 'doing okay'—I feel like I have been coping much better than I did after I lost Stephen. Wrong.

In hindsight, and after wrestling with chronic anxiety for a few weeks now I can see there were a lot of symptoms and warning signs leading up to this point, but, having never suffered from anxiety of these proportions before, I didn't realise what they were. Everything from severe nausea to seeing things out of the corner of my eye that weren't actually there, and everything in between.

I could write pages and pages of all the terrible symptoms and things I have been through in the past four weeks, but I fear that may bore you to tears. By far the worst experience out of all my symptoms, though, has been the intense belief that I am about to die.

Now I've always considered myself to be a fairly level-headed person who can deal with concerns (like the fact that none of us know how much time we have left on this earth) and move on. But my brain has been brutally malfunctioning, and the chemicals that can normally keep such concerns in check are out of balance and are causing me to focus on the things that terrify me the most, in spite of my best efforts. The panic attacks I have been having are triggered every time I hear of someone dying either by accident or illness (which seems to happen a lot - hence the anxiety). At times it has been so severe that I have a cold sensation come over my entire body and end up shaking, prostrate on my bed or in my chair, unable to move. It is terrifying. And the more intense the reaction, the more I can't help but believe I am reacting in that way because my body is telling me that I am about to die, which only makes the anxiety greater.

My psychologist tells me that the brain can't easily determine between reality and visualisation as non-reality. It's the reason we can get so swept up in the storyline of a good book or movie, or equally can feel deeply relaxed after a visual meditation exercise. But every positive has a flip side and unfortunately when we visualise some traumatic event our brain begins to respond as though the episode is actually occurring, and the body then dutifully follows.

Can you imagine it, Cec? Just close your eyes for a minute and imagine that you have just been told that you only have four weeks to live, and after that you know that your husband will be without his wife, and your precious children without their mother. How does it make you feel? For me, the idea is terrifying. Terrifying because I know it is a reality that people face every day. It is not that I fear death because I know I belong to Jesus, but it's the thought of my children and my husband having to go through such an enormous amount of suffering that completely brings me undone.

And it's all so unnecessary. As far as I am aware (and I have been checked out fairly thoroughly because I have been so anxious), I am in perfect health. There is no earthly reason to think I will be going anywhere anytime soon. So why would I put myself through such anxiety? There is no reason, and I keep trying to remind myself of that. It's not that a 'premature death' will never happen; it may or it may not. But there is absolutely nothing I can do about it if it does, and there is no advantage to worrying about something that I have no reliable indication will happen. In fact I found a great quote this week from Corrie ten Boom that says, "Worry does not empty tomorrow of its sorrow; it empties today of its strength."

That is precisely how all of this is making me feel. I know it's anxiety and not reality. Even if I was to die young, I don't believe that this anxiety is my body warning me of it. It's my mind playing tricks on me and it is awful. It has sapped me of my strength and it is robbing me of my hope. I can't enjoy time with my husband or time with my children because constantly in the back of my mind is the thought; "what if this is the last time your husband kisses you?" or; "what if you don't live to pick your daughter up from school this afternoon?"

In short, I am a mess. A quivering, shaking, lame excuse for a person. Admittedly the anxiety is not all day, every day. On the worst days I may suffer acutely for several hours and then start to have some relief. On the better days I begin to feel a little more normal and can put my concerns out of my mind. But that is usually when it hits. Having spoken with a few people recently who suffer from anxiety, this seems to be quite common. It doesn't get you when you're down so much—it gets you when you are coping. That's one of the reasons it's so terrifying; because it catches you off guard. More than that, it can create anxiety all of its own. When you are doing well you can become anxious about an impending attack of anxiety.

And I feel stupid. I have to keep reminding myself that I have been through a hugely traumatic few years, and that I am not well. I do need to rest and I do need to protect my heart. But this can be very hard to remember especially when I do start to feel like I am having a better coping day. I'm also frustrated and depressed because I know I will likely have many, many more months ahead of dealing with this, as well as other facets of the grief process. I feel like I should be an expert on grief, but what I actually feel is a novice. Everything seems as new and as awful as it did after losing Stephen. I feel like so many other people have had great insights into grief and that I am just full of crap. Useless, sentimental, unhelpful crap.

Which is another reason why I am feeling very insecure about what I wrote earlier. The more my life rolls on, the less I am confident about what I think I know and the more I feel an inclination to shut my mouth all together.

I also can relate a little to your friend who has suffered trauma after trauma and how she feels. I also feel like I am not coping very well and that God is not doing much to help me. Last night I read about half of C.S. Lewis' *A Grief Observed* which was good because it showed me that that was exactly how he felt too, but also bad because his wife died of cancer. The whole cancer thing set me off on another panic attack and I had to put the book down. Every time I have had a cough, sniffle or headache in the past four weeks I begin convincing myself it's cancer, and it takes an enormous amount of strength to then convince myself otherwise. Even I can see the comical side to this, but I'm not really at a place yet that I can laugh at myself.

So the one thing I ask of you in your reply is not to talk about people with cancer or people dying prematurely. I can't cope at the moment. On the other hand, feel free to make me laugh. I need a good laugh. An embarrassing moment, an hilarious anecdote; I could use some hope and cheerfulness.

Sorry for the depressing letter.

Hannah

P.S. In spite of the doom and gloom in my life, your inventory of culinary creations facilitated by your Thermomix™ actually brightened my day. To begin with I am stoked that you have such a useful tool to help you meet the overwhelming challenges of catering for your family. On a more selfish level I don't feel so silly in imagining an appliance that was born out of a love affair between a slow cooker and an ice cream maker.

-10-

Dear Hannah,

I feel guilty. You wrote me a very honest, candid letter, full of all sorts of pain and sadness and it is now more than a month later and I have still not replied.

I had good intentions. Not that they count for much.

I also had a few things going on, like finishing my novel, about which I was obsessively intense, and the fact that my RSI has been playing up as well and my shoulders and arms hurt for much of the day, so I wanted to keep my computer time for doing what I considered the urgent things (i.e. the novel) but if I am completely honest, those things are not really the reason that I haven't written back.

The truth is, it felt too hard.

I knew I had to produce 2,000 or so meaningful, coherent, wise, compassionate, well-written words on a topic that isn't funny, clever or cute in order to further a relationship with a person that I care about (i.e. you) and I didn't want to stuff it up.

I may yet stuff it up.

Perhaps this is the really difficult thing about grief. It can hamper relationships just because it is so big and painful that people don't really know what to do with it. For me, it is easier to put off writing an important letter then to take the risk that I might write it badly or wrong.

Also, and here is where my voice tapers off into a vague mumble, *I kinda got bored*. And then, I kinda got scared.

Because, and I say this all embarrassed and cringing, in the last six weeks I have seen, growing up in my own heart, the beginnings of attitudes of boredom, hardness and a teensy amount of victim-blaming masquerading as self-justification.

Which scares the heck out of me.

I don't want to be a Job's friend. And I have had enough people give me pat answers and clichés in response to my own pain that I never want to do it to anyone else. But this month, with an exciting novel to write, a blog to create and craft to make for a school fete stall, I guiltily chose the fun, interesting, happy stuff over the more painful, other-centred, difficult stuff. And left your letter off the list.

Of course, I can justify myself by saying that everyone else would do the same thing, that I'm not that unusual, and that you can't blame me for wanting to stay within my (self-imposed) deadline for my novel, and that people who don't have RSI don't know how painful it is, and of course all that is mostly true, but it doesn't stop the fact that my heart turned away from love.

Love is patient, love is kind, love does not envy, love is long-suffering, *yada yada yada*. I know the passage well. I speak on it. And yet, it is the hardest thing of all to put into practice, especially when things are boring.

And on that point, I wonder if you would disagree with me, Hannah, that grief is boring. Uninteresting. Dull. Blah.

I'm not even talking about other people's grief (and, let's face it, most of other people's stuff—happiness, grief, whatever—is never as interesting as our own). I'm talking about my own tears and pains and anxieties and reactions.

It was boring being homesick every night at boarding school when I was eleven. I got so that I found a way to block out the misery and just go to sleep after nine or ten weeks of nightly wet pillows.

It was tedious crying about missing Pakistan and always feeling like an outsider as an older teen and young adult when our family came back to Australia. 'Re-entry' grief got boring after I'd had a couple of years of it. I boxed up the feelings and moved them out of the lounge room of my psyche into a back bedroom and then eventually out on to the veranda.

Being devastated and sad about my son having autism was also boring. It was annoying to myself that I wanted to talk about nothing else, that my conversation and interests went around and around in smaller and smaller circles. I prided myself on my ability to converse with anyone about anything, never letting things get awkward or uncomfortable. It was so dull, doing nothing but therapy and dealing with tantrums day after day after day, always coming up against the same old feelings and reactions and beliefs.

I find my own grief boring. It tears the soul out of me and rips me apart. Sometimes, when it feels like pain will never end and I'll be stuck there forever, I just want to shovel it all away and run off to a brighter climate and more exotic beachfront location where it can't follow me.

When I enter into someone else's pain, it feels exciting for a little while. I get to exercise lovely, compassionate facial expressions that I'm quite good at really and listen effectively, nodding knowingly, but really thinking that *I'm doing the right thing, and people will really like me for this.* Of course, in my unspoken thoughts, I have time limits.

I'm such an impatient and unkind creature. I want you to feel better and be 'all fixed' (say that with a bright, fake, sparkly smile for maximum impact) according to my schedule so that I will feel better and not feel bad and guilty for not answering your letter because I'm too lazy and too uncaring to enter back into the world of pain you're living in right now, even for the short hour it will take me to write this.

When the shoe's on the other foot, though, and I'm the one hurting, I am devastated when people treat me like I treat them. If I'm sad or grieving and my husband doesn't say the exact right thing at the exact right time, he's toast. And I mean burned toast.

I have extremely uncharitable thoughts about people who don't give me appropriate support, who say unhelpful things and who dare to 'get on' with their lives while I'm still floundering around in grief and pain.

And then I find, to my shame and disappointment, that I'm exactly the same.

All of this underscores *again* for me that people—and I basically mean myself—do not love others. We can be *nice*, some of us know how to do *charming* and many of us appear to be caring, at least for a little while. But when 'love' requires sustained patience, kindness, perseverance and the other stuff that goes along with it, we give up and go on to more exciting things.

Love, and I mean love in its constituent parts—the patience, kindness, letting go of grudges, forgiveness, perseverance—is the greatest challenge of my life. I am defeated again and again by it. And yet I am elated when it is given to me.

You may have noticed that I rarely refer to bible verses in my writing. I avoid it because I think that often it's too easy to give 'Sunday school' answers and avoid doing your own thinking. Today, however, I can see the state of my own heart, and it's not pretty. I am pushed (hard) back to rely on grace, on God's love, which is so much better than my own.

> *...because of the great love with which [God] loved us, even when we were dead in our trespasses, [he] made us alive together with Christ...* [1]

Hannah, I apologise for my inability to love you perfectly, to show you patience, kindness and perseverance with no schedule and no time limits. I can't do it on my own. All I can do is accept God's more perfect love for me and let him change my heart and my thoughts.

If you still want to write back, I'll be interested (and I mean it) in hearing how the anxiety is going, and how you're going with all your new author-type endeavours. I'm also

---

[1] Ephesians 2:4-5

extremely interested in discussing something I read in one of your recent blog posts, the need to be validated.

With God's love, because my own is pretty rubbish,

Cecily

-11-

Dear Cecily,

I am finding this correspondence challenging. Not for the first time since we started this series of letters I have wanted to call you and discuss things with you over the phone or meet with you in person because sometimes I think it is better to talk about things face to face. But knowing that our aim is to eventually publish these letters for others to read I find myself faced with the task of trying to write my thoughts to you rather than having a heart-to-heart in person.

Actually, I am wondering if it is this very issue that is causing me some of the heartache from what you have written; the awareness of writing to a greater audience rather than just responding to little old me. Because quite honestly Cecily, I can't imagine for a moment that if I had poured out all of the emotion and the hardship of my last letter to you in person that your response would have been as it was in your last letter.

This is very hard for me to say. By nature I am an encourager. I like to find the good and positive in things people do and build them up. But the trouble is that sometimes I sacrifice the truth—truth that may hurt but will probably help someone to grow as a person—for the sake of encouragement. Instinctively that is what I want to do in this very letter; to gloss over the things that have upset me and to move on and focus on what was good. But I feel that would be taking the easy way out.

It's not that what you wrote upset me. I think you make some very honest observations about yourself and the state of the human heart in general. I also agree with you that grief and suffering can be a bit boring. But I think it was what you *didn't* write that has upset me.

My last letter to you was written by a woman who was suffering a whole new world of hurt unlike any she'd experienced before. Yes, it was a long letter, and perhaps it got a little boring and repetitive. But you're my friend. I expect you to be interested. And yes, there's that ugly word from several letters ago; expectation.

I am not in the least bit bothered by the fact that you have taken a long time to reply to my last letter, or even by the fact that you have been putting it off because it was hard and there were far more other interesting things in your life. You have your own family, your own responsibilities, your own work. I don't expect you to make me and my pain a priority above those things. But when you did eventually sit and write to me I would have loved it if you had engaged in my world a little, even just a smidge, just so there was some encouragement and empathy.

In my last letter I really wanted to give you some encouragement about how you are parenting, and I find that I am left hanging a little. I have no idea whether or not you found my encouragement encouraging. I'm cool with the feedback that it wasn't (if it wasn't), but I'm really finding it hard to have no indication whatsoever. It leaves me feeling a bit foolish. I'm not sure if you didn't make mention of it because it was unhelpful, unimportant, ridiculous or boring. How will I know whether or not to venture my encouragement in future?

But I suppose the thing I found the hardest was the way in which your letter left me feeling like I only had two options from that point forward; to change the topic or to cease writing. I know that you said towards the end you would be interested to hear about how I was going, but it was sorta hard to believe you meant it when you had just finished writing about how boring it can be feeling grief and listening to others going through it.

I really appreciate your honesty; I always appreciate honesty. But I think you could have said everything you did, felt the way you felt, and still encouraged me and shown me love. But perhaps you got so freaked out about how badly you felt you were reacting that you forgot you could still do something about it, even in that moment.

I'll say it again, Cec, this is not an easy letter for me to write. I can see that the Lord has been challenging your heart lately, and it is for this reason that I do write honestly. Hardness of heart is something that we all suffer with in varying degrees, all of the time. The trouble is that often we don't see just how hard we are because the people in our lives are not willing to tell us when we have failed, or at least not usually in a constructive and deliberate way.

I'm all for grace and understanding in relationships, but if I had really missed the mark or caused major offence to a friend I would sincerely want to know about it so I could reconcile and hopefully learn something of benefit, regardless of whether or not I felt justified in what I'd said or how I'd acted. I'm going out on a limb with this letter in the hope that you may feel the same way.

It's funny how you wanted to talk about the validation theme I recently wrote about in my blog. I suppose that is what I felt was missing from your last letter. You didn't have to fix all my problems or even come up with helpful or insightful remarks. If you had nothing to offer beyond a simple understanding of the fact that this place I am at in my life is extremely difficult and that you still wanted to be my friend through it all, it would have been enough.

It is difficult to love as Christ did; impossible to do it consistently. I came to this realisation myself some time ago when I thought I had just done the most godly, generous and charitable thing for someone else, and I felt the conviction that if I was really honest with myself, I had done it to feel good about serving God rather than just doing it from a place of love. It got me thinking about how all sorts of gestures, grand and small, made in the name of love, so often have selfish motives attached. It's not pretty.

I've heard a statistic that says on average it takes seven years for a couple to begin doing things totally out of love and selflessness for the benefit of the other. I would agree with that, and even add that when it begins to happen, it is only the start of a life-long process. And that's just with the person we love and are devoted to above all (well, second in line to God that is). So imagine what it's like for other relationships which are further down the pecking order. Again, it's not pretty.

We all suffer from it, Cec, but I am confident of this very thing; that he who began a good work in you will perfect it until the day of Christ Jesus (Philippians 4:6).

I do love you, Cec, albeit imperfectly. I will gladly accept your imperfect love if you will accept mine. How 'bout it?

Hannah

-12-

Dear Hannah,

You are completely right. About everything. And I apologise wholeheartedly. Not for what I wrote but, as you said, for what I *didn't* write.

I wanted to be honest, not just for myself, but also for our wider audience (which I kind of wish wasn't there sometimes). Ironically, I left you out of the picture almost entirely, and for that I'm very, very sorry.

If I could write the last letter again, I'd say this:

My dear friend, it must be horrendous to experience panic and anxiety so extreme that it feels like it's completely out of your control. There is almost nothing to say that can possibly help. I've had depression but never anxiety or panic attacks and the levels you are experiencing sound absolutely debilitating.

If I was with you in person, I'd probably ask you more questions about it so I could understand it a little better. I'd shake my head and make *tsk tsk* noises on my tongue about it because it seems so unfair and so much more difficult to deal with the aftermath of tragedy than even the tragedy itself. I'd probably also join you in a piece of sticky chocolate cake because I'd reckon that might help alleviate some of the fear and physical distress.

I also appreciate your encouragement of my parenting, even despite your own difficulties. And for that I say a big thank you. Whenever *anyone* tells me I'm doing a reasonable job I'm grateful—almost ridiculously so. I find parenting so extremely challenging that I wear my mother guilt around like a poncho sometimes. Nothing's ever good enough, and I've never done enough and surely they're all going to need serious amounts of therapy when they're 30 or so unless I do better today and tomorrow and the next day after that.

What I missed in my silly, self-absorbed letter was the very thing I asked you about: validation. God knows (he really does) that validation is what I most crave in just about everything I do. (I mean, why else post countless pictures of sourdough loaves on Facebook? For that matter, why post anything on Facebook?) In exploring my own heart I completely neglected to validate yours.

Here, I offer the validation that I selfishly left out of my letter.

You have experienced a double-whammy set of tragedies. What makes them worse is that they were both the same type of dreaded worst-case scenarios, one after the other in quick succession, without time for recovery (if there is in fact any recovery possible when a baby or child dies.)

You suffered great pain at both times.

You continue to suffer, in expected and unexpected ways, as a result of the trauma caused by the tragedies.

Your mind is suffering, your thought life is suffering, your very purpose and plans for your life have been shattered and there is enormous (often unrecognized) suffering in that.

Your body is suffering physically. All your systems have had huge stress placed on them and your physical existence is challenged in ways that no one really understands, especially not yourself. Your physical body seems out of your control and that brings a certain level of fear and confusion that only adds to the discomfort.

Life around you carries on when (I imagine) what you want is for it to slow down and stop and see you and how you are living and what you've been through. Not forever, but just enough to say, "You matter, you're an important part of this universe. You are loved."

You said in letter 9 this: "I feel like I am not coping very well and that God is not doing much to help me."

I totally get how you feel. In my days of chaos and crazy when my son with autism was at his most manic I used to put my head down on the kitchen bench in despair and pray, "You've got to help me! I can't do this!"

I wasn't coping well. But I'm not sure that *anyone* copes well with most hard things. Not really. Even if we look like we do, we feel like we aren't.

And unfortunately, as you say, it felt like God wasn't listening. I didn't get a magic zoom of energy or sudden wisdom or a lifting of the fog. Instead it felt like I just had to work harder myself and pull myself up by my socks to find that little bit more strength to finish the day. I still feel a little cynical when I read blog posts or books which give the line, 'Well, if you're impatient, or unloving or whatever, you just need to pray more and read the Bible and God will hear you and change things.'

And it sounds like as long as you do those two things, everything will just work out without having to do anything else. Bah humbug. It may be true for some, but I'll bet it's not the answer for a lot of folk. We're just all too nervous to say it.

I believe God *did* help me. It just wasn't in the way I expected him to.

I believe God put things in front of me that helped; good therapy for my son, really useful books about emotions and feelings, parenting principles I'd never seen before, the right doctor who knew what she was doing. I would feel out of control and out of my depth and within the month or two, there would be something that either popped out to me on a library shelf, or someone who gave me a contact, or something I discovered on the internet that I could see would help.

Mind you, none of those things provided have been easy to do. Not one single bit.

The therapy took massive amounts of money, time and a complete change of parenting philosophy. I felt disheveled by the changes I had to go through internally in order to do it.

The emotional management required going deeply into my internal beliefs and self-talk and making big changes there. It was painful and disorderly and, again, expensive. I didn't enjoy it.

The parenting changes required me to plant and grow the tiny, delicate seeds of patience and kindness that I would have preferred to ignore. I will not lie. I find patience painful and, yes, boring to learn. But as the plants grow and I reap the fruit, I can see the benefits to all of us. (Even just yesterday, I was able to negotiate a difficult afternoon where I was insulted by my son for pretty much four hours straight without losing my cool or being overcome by it. My patience muscles are pretty big these days.)

The medical changes took me to a whole other level in so many ways. I now have way more knowledge about nutrition and cooking than I ever desired to have. And I'm an expert in feeding difficult eaters. Getting fussy autistic kids to eat vegetables is not a job for the fainthearted. And feeding your child fourteen different supplements per day costs so much that I've had to learn to economise in every area of life.

So God did change things for me, and my son. But it was the slow, hard, boring way. Bit by bit, teeny tiny step by teeny tiny step. I look back at it, and I'm almost (not quite) grateful that he did it that way because I'm not so sure that having a miracle story ("Look, God fixed it all!") is necessarily the most encouraging one for other people who might not get a miracle either.

I suspect that this is the way he will do it for you too. And there will be many more times that you will feel bad and as if he's not helping. All I can say is that it's a really hard feeling to have. It's not fun. It's not pretty. And I know how it feels, a little bit.

Hannah, I am really sorry for my previous letter. And I'm grateful to you for writing to me as you did. I'm sorry to give you extra stress in your day, worrying about whether you should have written it or not. You did absolutely the right thing and I appreciate it.

Hey, you know, why don't we just go out for a coffee and chocolate cake soonish?

Cecily

-13-

Hiya Cec,

It has been so long since I've written. Your last letter was sent to me just over two months ago. Although I did send you a little email at the time to let you know that I got it and all was well, I haven't been able to write back to you since then because of my depression. I was sucked into the dark vortex even more so in the past six weeks, but am glad to report that I think I have begun to see light at the end of the tunnel. And thankfully, it's not a train.

I loved your last letter so much. I loved it because of the validation and the insight you shared, but even more than that, I loved it because of your humility and ability to hear someone when they said, "Hey, I thought you didn't do that very well," take it on board, apologise and change. From the very first time I read one of your books I already suspected you would be this type of woman. But I have been wrong before.

I've met so many people who ask to be held accountable or want to have an 'open and honest' friendship so that people can 'speak into their lives' when they see something of concern. And I'm not even talking about the people who have done it carelessly or without prayerful consideration. I'm talking about people who have approached said friends with genuine care, love, hurt or concern, and have been slammed into the ground for their trouble.

Thank you for being a woman who not only talks the talk, but walks the walk. I love you for it.

The last few months have been a time of much growth and learning on my part. I have just been moseying on, trying to get through each day in one piece, waiting on God to show me what he wants to, and waiting on myself to get better. In this sort of companionable spiritual silence (I have been praying about lots of other things, but not about myself), God has revealed to me a few little gems.

I wholeheartedly agree with this statement from your last letter, when you said: "I believe God *did* help me. It just wasn't in the way I expected him to."

I think God has been showing me the sorts of ways he has been helping me, and he has also unearthed a very poor theology I had created for myself over the course of my life.

I somehow had come to a point of thinking that in order for an action to be a God-directed, special 'looking after me' and 'loving me' thing, it had to be something specific he had directed to be done. This might mean that if someone brought me a book or sent me a bible verse, that it wasn't really 'from God' if they hadn't heard a big, loud voice in the sky telling them to do that for me. This might also mean that any sort of healing, if it was to come from God, had to be a supernatural event.

No wonder I've spent so many years confused.

What God has shown me is that although he *can* do these things and he *does* indeed do them from time to time, that one of the biggest expressions of his love is through his church; the body of Christ. Every person who has prayed for me, cooked me a meal, given me a gift, sent me a verse (yes, even the clumsy ones) have all been God showing me his love. What I failed to understand is that although these things may not have been because of a specific 'Yes, sir' order from above, they came about as people demonstrated their testimony of God's love in their own lives as they served me in Jesus' name.

I have this vision of you sitting at your desk as you read this with your palm smacked on your head, and the words, "well, derrr" on your lips. And rightly so. It seems a fairly fundamental blunder. But I wonder how many other people get themselves into the same tangle I did about the way in which God expresses his love.

Part of the trouble is that we say things all the time such as, "we are all part of the body and we serve each other out of love," but it sounds more like a responsibility that we have to each other rather than a powerful testimony of what God has done in us. Loving and sacrificially serving each other is purely an extension of our adoration and worship of God. It has only just dawned on me what a gift it is to be part of the body of Christ, not merely because I get taken care of, but because I get to experience and witness God's love in the lives of others who truly know him.

Anyway, the good news is that I think I am starting to get better. It's even a little unnerving. I've been feeling wretched for so long that I'm finding it hard to know what to do with myself now that I feel like doing something.

Actually, that's an outright lie. I am by no means short of things to be doing, or things that I want to do. I think I shall have to be patient though. My energy is still very low, so I shall have to find the balance between getting jobs done and still giving myself chance to recover. I suspect it's like when you recover from a really bad flu; you start to feel that little bit better and you tackle a big project or outing 'cause you're on top of the world, only to find that you are still pretty wiped out and the only reason you thought you felt as good as you did was because you have been feeling SO bad that even a small improvement makes you feel like Lazarus. After he was raised from the dead, that is. Well, you know what I mean.

So I am wondering how things are in the Paterson house at present? I see on Facebook you have been busy with speaking engagements, and your son with ASD has a bit of a fixation with death threats. How are you all going? I can't believe it's school holidays again in another few weeks. Are you looking forward to them or dreading them, or a mixture of both?

In other news, I visited my sister on the weekend. You'll never guess what she's just bought. A Thermomix™. She cooked all sorts of delicious treats for us. It's a pretty fine contraption, although I must say it is a bit noisy, especially when it is set up only inches from where you are sleeping on the family room floor on an air mattress. But I can see it makes life a lot easier for her, so that makes me happy.

I must run as I have children to bath before dinner. They taste terrible if you don't wash them first.

Much love to you and yours,

Hannah xo

-14-

Dear Hannah,

It's funny, isn't it, how we create these ideas of what we think God ought to do for us. I grew up in a Christian home always hearing that 'God answers prayers'. At the age of about six I began to think more about this and God in general, usually when I was sitting on the toilet and had run out of other interesting things to do while I waited to complete my business. (I must either have been really constipated or really impatient because these days it doesn't take all that long. Sorry, too much information.)

Anyhow, while toileting and thinking one day about the big questions of life, I noticed a small rock on the floor of the bathroom. I don't know why it was there. It certainly wasn't part of the décor. But it triggered an idea as I sat there with my pants around my ankles.

I could test out this 'God answers prayers' thing.

"Dear God," I began, quite politely. "If you're real, prove it to me by moving that rock. You don't have to move it far. Just an inch or so. Amen."

And then I sat and watched and waited.

And of course, the rock didn't move.

I wiped my bottom, got off the toilet and pondered my options.

First, I felt annoyed and slightly affronted. Why *wouldn't* God move the rock for me? It's not like it would have been a big problem for him. I felt as though I would be quite within my rights to declare poutily that God was in fact, not at all real. I was almost enjoying my feelings of affront and disappointment.

Even while I was stomping around, hands on hips, telling myself that God probably wasn't there at all, I heard a niggling voice of reason in the back of my brain.

"He didn't *have* to move that rock, silly. He knows you'll believe in him anyway, without pointless miracles for proof. Plus, he's got more important things to do." (Actually, I probably didn't use the word 'pointless' at the age of six.)

As an adult I don't go around asking God to move tiny rocks for me, but I do have a few more grown up equivalents which sound a bit like yours. When I'm feeling particularly down I often think that all I want is for some of my more spiritually-minded, 'in tune with God' type friends to send me a message saying, "Hey, Cecily, I really feel that I need to say this to you. . ." or, "I was moved to pray specifically for you at such and such a time."

Because wouldn't that just prove, once and for all, not only that God exists, but that he actually, genuinely cares personally for me? That's the bit I struggle with—that God is bothered with the details of my small life. I've always been one to see the big picture of God's work in the world. The Spread of the Gospel. The Doing of Good. Those things are great, of course. But it's hard to hold that view together with the thought that God actually cares enough about me to be there with me when I feel like crying.

And yes, I have cried recently. It was the school holidays that did it. I love my children, but in the fortnight that they had off school they did not live up to the 'happy families' ideal that I like to carry around in my head .

I have one child who picks fights with his siblings wherever he goes, another whose 'buttons' have a hair trigger and a three year-old who might possibly be hyperactive and who talks pretty much 12 hours a day. To me. Which is hard to deal with, especially when you're at the beach with five good books and all you want to do is sleep and read and NOT cook and NOT answer questions and NOT play princesses. Oh, I also have a teenage daughter, but the less we say about *that* the better.

So after two weeks I was worn down. Exhausted. Destroyed. I cheered, actually quite loudly, after they all went back to school. I even put the little one in to preschool for an extra day just so I could have six hours to myself without interruption. And it was nice.

I think you're smart to 'wait' to get better. Lots of things (most things?) get better with time. Even feeling worn out from school holidays gets better with time.

It's just a pain to wait, especially if you're a goer with lots of ideas which I am, and which I think you are too. When I have to wait it feels like I'm wasting my life. But sometimes we just need to accept how we feel, live with it, let it be, and wait. Because next week will be a little better, and the month after that will be even better and maybe next year we'll have forgotten about just how terrible and tragic we were because things seem to be normal. There will always be times of sadness and mourning, probably that will recur fairly regularly, but there does come a time when the cloud lifts and the sunlight comes back in and the plants of life and love begin to grow again.

Plus in my case, my moods swing. Crazy-wild. I can be ready to hurt someone on Monday, in tears of desperation on Wednesday and then busy, excited and making new plans on Saturday. Gotta love those hormones.

I'm actually beginning to see waiting as a blessing. If I can speak enough sense to myself on the days when I feel that I'm entirely alone and misunderstood and tragic, I can journal it to get it out, but then wait, knowing that I'm more than likely going to feel so much better in a week that I'll look back and say, "What? Really?"

How is your waiting going? Are you pacing yourself? Don't take lessons from me in living a moderate life. This school term I'm running a craft stall at our school fete, decorating for my brother's wedding, sewing (with a friend) 28 yellow and red unitards as costumes for our school musical, helping at the school musical, publishing a new book and sub-editing someone else's book. Oh, and there's also Christmas, with Carols (I play the trumpet), a ginger bread house making night and presents to organize. Ridiculous. But will I get rid of anything? Um, no.

Love, Cecily x

-15-

Dear Cecily,

You'll be pleased to know that now every time I think about why God hasn't answered my prayers I have an image of you as a kid sitting on your toilet doing a poo. But the lesson has stuck, which I am grateful for.

Sounds like your holidays were pretty rough, and in some sense just plain cruel. The very fact that you mentioned a pile of books to read and a deck chair suggests you had some definite expectations of what your holiday would be like. It seems cruel that you were was robbed of them. I am very sorry that it was such a hard slog. That being said, did you perhaps have a teeny-weeny, little bit too high an expectation—with one pre-teen child with Autism, a teenage daughter we won't speak of, a seven year-old son and a preschooler who can't stop talking—that you might even be able to sit your bum down for more than five minutes, let alone get through a stack of books? Just a thought.

And yes, I heard the shout of joy from here. I hope you don't feel guilty about it. Kids are hard work.

Now for something hilarious. In my last letter, which I wrote almost three months ago, I talked about God not giving great signs. In your reply you talked about the ebbs and flows of ideas and creativity, and going from doing nothing and waiting to feel better to being totally swamped and going for it. I want you to keep both of these ideas in mind as I tell you what has happened in the past two months. Because the irony is amazing.

At the end of August my husband took me on a two-night getaway to the Blue Mountains for our wedding anniversary. It was the first time we had really been away from home and the kids since we lost Esther, and, as a result, it was the first time all year that I think my mind was able to have a break from the doom and gloom and actually start looking towards a future. Because as you know, being able to envisage any sort of future when your plans have been so radically changed and you are mourning the loss of them is almost impossible.

So there I was relaxing in a spa bath with my husband (that image is just to get back at you for the toilet story). I lay there in hot bubbly bliss thinking to myself, *if I could choose anything in the world I would like to do with my time, what would it be?*

I was staggered to find the answer was already in my mind. It came to me as soon as I'd had that thought. It also astounded me because I don't ever remember thinking it before, but as soon as it came to me it made so much sense.

Now don't laugh. It's a hard thing for me to tell people. I'm worried that people will look at me and say, "You're out of your mind! You can't pull that off!"

So here goes.

If I could be anything in the world that I wanted to be, it would be *a stand-up comedian*.

There, I said it.

Thoughts? Comments?

In the absence of immediate communication after this revelation, I shall press on and tell you more.

As soon as this idea came into my head it was as if a light-bulb went on in my mind. I've always struggled with what I should do with my life. I have a very unique skill set (music performance, public speaking, writing funny poems, graphic design, event management), and although I have found jobs and outlets in my life to be able to enjoy or make use of these things, I've never really found something that seemed to make use of all of them.

That is, until now.

It was almost as if the idea set off a chain reaction in my brain and every single skill, gift, interest and ability I have ever pursued in my life clicked into place. I started to get an idea that this is what God had in mind for me all along.

But hold the phone a moment.

Hmmmm. God. Ah yes, a slight blip in the plan. What did God have to think about all of this? I have to be truthful and say that as soon as the stand-up comedian idea came into my mind it was immediately followed by a subtext. *I would love to be a stand-up comedian. . . to encourage Christians in their faith and remind them that God does want them to have joy in their lives.*

That was my desire and design right from the start. And quite frankly, something I felt was a worthy one. Yet I also know how many times in my life I have thought big thoughts and ideas in the name of spreading the gospel, but they really haven't been God's plan for me.

Well I know you know what it's like to have an idea that you are so excited about that your brain just can't put it down. I was like a kid with a shiny new toy, and unfortunately for my husband I think my head was in the clouds for the rest of our time away together. I was on overload with ideas and possibilities for my new career. His loving attempts to make conversation with his wife were just plain distracting. Well, not really, but you get the point.

The more I thought about it, the more excited I became. And the more excited I got, the more I didn't want to pray about it because I was worried that God was going to say "no" and take away my shiny new toy.

So I didn't. I deliberately put off praying about it for a full week. I just wanted to live out the fantasy in my own mind before I let God say no.

During that first week I had only confided in my husband. I was (and still am) so paranoid that people will laugh at the idea (and not in a good way) that I didn't want to tell anyone else. But after about six days I was chatting to my mum and I thought I would test the waters.

I told her about the idea I had and she seemed excited and supportive. At the end of the conversation she said to me, "How can I pray for you in this situation?"

"No! Don't do that!" I fired back. Then I got the guilts. I realised the time had come where I really did need to pray about it because if it was not something I was to pursue I needed to turn my mind towards other things.

So I said to her, "Well actually, yes you could pray for me. Perhaps you could just pray that if this is the path for me to travel that God would make that abundantly clear."

The following day I knew my mother had prayed because of what happened next.

We have a sponsor child in Indonesia and there is about a two month time lag between letters written and delivered. The very next morning I checked my letterbox and there was a letter from Kiki.

I opened it up and read all about his school and family which was all very lovely as usual. But I almost fell over laughing when I flipped the letter over. On the bottom section of the back page of the form there is a big white box where the children can draw pictures. And in the box, completely unrelated to anything that was written in his letter, Kiki had drawn a picture of a single microphone on a stand and the words STAND UP COMEDY written in big bubble letters right next to it.

Which is amazing, because God doesn't really do those sorts of signs for me, right?

Well, just in case there was any doubt in my mind as to God's resounding YES in answer to my question, he sent me another message via the mail later that afternoon as well. (Who knew God relied on Australia Post?).

My sister, who at the time was totally unaware of any of these things, had a few weeks earlier ordered me a hand-made piece of jewellery simply as an 'I love you and am thinking of you' gift. Have I mentioned that I love my sister dearly?

Anyhow, I had no idea that this was on its way and I opened the package to find a beautifully personalised message on the pendant she had made for me. It was a bible reference from the book of Philemon. (Admittedly I had forgotten that there was even a book in the bible called Philemon, so the verse didn't automatically come to my mind.)

> *I thank my God always when I remember you in my prayers, because I hear of your love and of the faith that you have toward the Lord Jesus and for all the saints, and **I pray that the sharing of your faith may become effective for the full knowledge of every good thing that is in us for the sake of Christ. For I have derived much joy and comfort from your love, my brother, because the hearts of the saints have been refreshed through you.** Philemon 1:4-7 ESV (emphasis mine)*

Two things happened when I read this. First of all I almost wet my pants with excitement. And secondly, I started making plans and I haven't looked back.

Don't take lessons from me for living a moderate lifestyle either. My waiting is finally over and I am in overdrive! In the past eight weeks I have booked or am in the process of booking 24 venues across two states for a new stand-up comedy show that I have also half written in that time. I have been organising and designing flyers, posters, tickets, websites and book covers, and have had all the joy of dealing with twenty-four separate venues and their individual hire arrangements and negotiating fees.

I am also desperately trying to get two books finished either before or near to Christmas, and we are almost halfway through November. In amongst all of that I have been designing websites for some other clients, helping my husband with his final assessments for a course he has been doing, and trying not to forget that I have two living children and two living parents who occasionally like to see me and who, as I've discovered, do not always want to talk about my show.

So at the moment, flat out like a lizard drinking does not even begin to describe where I'm at. But I wouldn't have it any other way.

I've also learned that God knew that I would be like a racehorse out of the stalls as soon as he gave me this idea and that although I know he expects me not to get my priorities mixed up and not to neglect my family or friends, he is spurring me on in all I am doing. I could write a whole other letter telling you the amazing ways he is just going before me in everything I am doing in relation to this tour, paving the way. I am overwhelmed by his grace and love.

And that, my friend, is pretty much it.

I would love to hear how you are coping in the lead up to the silly season, especially with all of your jobs. How did your craft stall go? How are the unitards looking? I've never worn a unitard in my life, but my hat is off to those who dare.

With much love,

Hannah xo

-16-

Dear Hannah,

A few months ago I had your letter about being so miserable you pretty much couldn't do anything except crochet (not that there's anything wrong with crocheting; in fact, I'd quite like to take it up one day myself).

"Poor thing," I thought to myself. "I hope she can find something to focus on and put her energy into. But it'll probably still be a long ways off."

Then a few weeks ago I saw on Facebook that you had some new projects coming up.

"Hmm. I wonder what she's going to do?" I thought to myself. "Maybe some more books? Maybe a support group? Perhaps a charity?"

So I clicked on your link when you were ready to unveil, and there in front of me was an amusing caricature of you in front of a microphone and a title that said, *Hannah Boland, comedian.*

Okaaaaaay.

It was unexpected. But also, pretty funny as a concept. Which I guess is a good start for your career. If you can bring yourself to make the jokes, you've got an easy four minutes of ironic material about how you got yourself into this. If I was a ticket-purchasing punter, I'd be intrigued by the back story, which is as good a way as any to get people along, right?

The more I think about it, the more I think it could really work. And obviously God thinks so too. I love the stories about the sponsor child and the necklace. I'm like you; to get those sorts of affirmations makes me feel so much better about what I do.

If it makes you feel any better, I also tend to *not* pray about things I really, really want to do. Because the simple fact is, if for some odd reason God *didn't* want me to do it, I don't know if I could give it up. Actually, this whole topic of 'what does God want me to do?' kind of annoys me. It goes along with the idea that if he wants you to do something he'll open up the 'doors' and make it easy for you.

My experience is different. I've had to beat down a lot of doors and find alternative entrances. Sometimes I've even had to sneak under fences and scratch through bushes to get in.

Take, for example, my novel *Invisible*. To even find the time to write it, I had to seriously reorganize my life and make difficult choices about not mopping floors and such. (Actually, that particular decision probably wasn't that difficult...) Sometimes putting the words onto the screen felt like torture. If I'd been using a pen I would have tried to poke my own eyes out. It's not so easy to do that kind of damage with a keyboard.

Once it was written, the *really* hard work began. It was rejected by every Australian publisher except one and agents didn't even bother replying. (When I write that, it sounds glib. But every rejection was like a punch in the stomach and laid me low for two days.) The publishers who didn't reject it, didn't accept it. But they did suggest I rewrite it. So I did that. Twice. Then they said, "yes, we like it" and then they said, "sorry, no, we don't".

A year after I'd finished it, it looked like it was done for. In desperation I decided to do the unthinkable and publish it myself (a sure sign of an amateur, loser writer, I thought) so I put it out there for free on all the places you can download e-books.

At that point I was seriously doubting whether I should be spending all this time writing, and in fact, whether I should be writing fiction at all. Was it just a vanity thing? Did God really want me to be doing something else? Like, maybe, feeding the poor and hungry? Or just doing a better job of organizing Sunday School?

But then the letters started to come in from kids and adults who had read it. For one girl with dyslexia, it was the first book she'd ever read start to finish. For another, it gave her courage to stand up and find her own voice. One 70 year-old woman told me it opened up old wounds from her childhood but in a healing way.

And then a Christian teenager who had been struggling for a long time read it with her dad. She loved it so much that she went out and bought a journal to write down her feelings, just like the main character, Jazmine. When she came home and showed it to her dad, she turned it over to see that the name 'Jasmine' was written on the back. "I think that's God saying that he's with you," said her dad.

I think he was right.

That email was important for me. It means God is using my work and my writing, even though I haven't been sure about it and even despite it all being so hard. So I feel affirmed. And I'll also continue to break down entrances and find other ways to do what I'm passionate about, even if it seems like the doors aren't wide 'open'. (Actually, I'm always telling my kids to shut the doors because they let in the flies and mosquitoes. Perhaps there's something in that...)

So basically, I'm of the opinion that if you have a passion for something and you just can't let go of it and other people are mostly on board, it's more than likely that God will affirm it because after all, he made us with our loves and likes and energy and drive and *why wouldn't* he want us to use what he's given us?

I'm sure you will have doors to bash down as you organize a comedy show tour. So go ahead and get yourself a good sledgehammer. And I'm definitely *not* going to tell you to slow down and take it calmly because I can't stand it when people say that to me. You can rest for so long. And then you have to move!

Stretch! Pursue! Fly! Go for it. It will be amazing.

I will give you one piece of advice though... take some Bach's Rescue Remedy with you. When I speak in public I sometimes find I have an adrenaline drop halfway through and end up a bit shaky and wobbly, even though I'm not actually consciously nervous. I was telling this to a horsewoman friend of mine and she said, "You should get some Rescue Remedy. It's really good. I use it all the time when I'm doing eventing."

"Oh really?" I said. "How much do you take?"

She looked at me surprised. "Oh, it's not for me. I give it to the horse!"

Anyway. Horse or human, it helps. Stick some in your pocket for when you're on stage. If you need it, you can take it *and* tell the joke about it too. Win-win.

Now for a change of topic. You said I should probably give up my expectations of having any sort of holiday with my kids around. I agree. And I try. But there's something that's imprinted on your brain from childhood that says 'When You Are At The Beach, You Are On Holiday And It Is Your God-given Right To Relax and Read Lots of Books.'

It's the same expectation that we all have that when we're sick our mums will put us in bed and let us drink flat lemonade all day.

I think the worst thing about being sick as an adult is not being sick. It's dealing with the disappointment of the fact that Mummy is not there any more. She will not come to sit on the edge of your bed, stroke your head and say, "Oh, poor thing. How are you feeling?" There is no flat lemonade. And you can't stay in bed because if you do the kids won't get to school on time, or get dinner or do their homework, or stay alive in any functional way.

And the worst thing about going on 'holiday' (ha ha) as a parent is not that there isn't really any holiday, it's dealing with the parts of your brain that flash on in happy anticipation when they hear the word 'holiday' and don't flash off again until you've doused them with about three days worth of crying.

Bah humbug.

One day I will get a holiday. And on that holiday I will do the following: read, sleep, read, sleep, eat, eat, eat, *not cook*, read, sleep, read, sleep, surf and shop. And *no-one* and I mean No-one, will come between me and my book.

Love Cecily

PS. Are you still sad? Has the depression gone or is it sitting still and taking a little break behind the whirlwind of excitement? How are you balancing this odd period where everything's in flux again?

-17-

Dear Cecily,

Last night I had an idea (no don't worry, not another career change). I thought I might go through and read all our letters from start to present and see how our little project has been coming together. And in those few hours where I sat and read I went through a whole range of emotions including (and in no particular order) embarrassment, shock, sadness, laughter, self-reproach and satisfaction.

I was embarrassed when I read my first letter. I was embarrassed because I was so full of my own self-affirmation in what I thought I understood about God. I shudder to think about how I tried giving both myself and you a little sermon on how God requires obedience even in the dark times. And I remember your response to that—you said I was perhaps being a little hard on myself and perhaps weighing myself down with some guilt.

The funny thing is when I received your first letter back and I read this I was really quite annoyed with you. I was very put out that you would even presume to tell me that I didn't know what I was talking about. After all, *I am* a godly person, and *I am* the one who knows what it is to grieve the loss of two children. To be honest, I thought you were being quite fluffy and not holding to the true gospel message.

As the year has progressed I realise I have been in places emotionally and spiritually that I never thought it would have been possible to go. And looking back on your first piece of advice all those months ago I realise you were 100 per cent right. Our God is a loving God and smothers us in grace. I see now that while his desire for us is to live a holy life he also knows how impossible it is for us in this lifetime to do so. That was the whole point of Jesus coming in the way that he did. He allows us to be before the Father, warts and all, because the warts are only going to be removed when this life is done.

Being a Christian and a lover of Jesus is not about striving to do better and changing our behaviour. It's about loving God. And when we love God he gives us the desire to change, along with the grace and strength to change.

But let's not kid ourselves about this. We are so wicked that the changes he brings about in us are really just a scratch on the surface. They are an outward reflection of the bigger change that has gone on deep within our hearts, and for some those changes may seem huge on the surface, and for others they may not seem that significant at all.

I think this is why we may be very surprised when we get to heaven. I think we will see a lot of people in heaven who we didn't expect to see, and conversely I think we shall be missing a lot of people who we thought would be there.

So then I come to the next emotion I experienced as I re-read our letters—sadness. Reading about how some of my friends weren't really there for me, and reading about finishing decorating Esther's room and the depth of despair in the panic attacks brought me to tears. Quite frankly it has been a horrible year. If I was the swearing type I would say wholeheartedly it has been a shit year. Good thing I'm not the swearing type.

But I also realised how sad I still am when you wrote your PS in your last letter. You asked me how my sadness and depression was.

As far as the depression goes, I am well on the road to recovery. I came off the antidepressants a few weeks ago and it is so nice to be able to feel genuine happiness and laughter and fun again (also kind of crucial when one is writing a stand-up comedy show).

The flip side to that, albeit not necessarily a bad one, is that because I am able to feel again, I feel the depth of my sadness in a way I haven't felt for some months. The difference is that now I can have my cry, feel low, wait for a few hours and then generally be able to come out of it and be okay again. I couldn't do that a few months ago.

The antidepressants numbed everything. I was sad thinking about Esther and Stephen but it was an underlying constant sadness that would occasionally manifest itself in a small outburst.

Now, as you have astutely guessed, I have lots of exciting things going on to distract me. But when I stop and take a breath, or even if I am just passing the lovely photo of Esther I have hanging on my wall, I burst into sobs emanating from somewhere deep within and I become very sad very quickly. Even just writing this paragraph has sent me reaching for the tissue box at least twice.

I miss my babies so much, Cec. There is hurt and grief in my heart which actually doesn't feel any less than when I first learned that Stephen was going to die. In these moments of grief the pain is so acute and the yearning so deep I wonder if it will ever really lessen. But the difference is now I am well enough to not let it take over my life. I can feel the sad, have my moment/s of utter crushing grief and then move into a different space. I couldn't do that a few months ago.

There are a few people in my life at the moment who are expecting babies. After Stephen died, pregnant mums and newborn babies really didn't worry me too much. I think that was because I had known from halfway through the pregnancy that I wouldn't have Stephen for very long and I had time to get used to the idea.

But this time it is so different. Every time I hear another pregnancy announcement or see an ultrasound picture on Facebook I am on the verge of bitterness. Let's call it extreme resentment. The rational part of my brain wants to tell my friends and family that I am genuinely happy for them and I wish them all the best (which I am sure on some level I do). But the emotional part of my brain just wants to say, SCREW YOU AND YOUR BABY! THIS IS SO UNFAIR!

There is a family member who is expecting her third baby right around the one year anniversary of Esther's birth/death and I am not coping well. When the news reached us earlier this year I had a minor meltdown but somehow managed to find that spot within me of genuine happiness in order to see the family and congratulate them. However since then I have managed to avoid seeing them.

The thought of seeing this lovely mum with another pregnant bump grieves me to my core. It is just so unfair.

Of course it's compounded by that fact that we are now in the lead up to Christmas so the whole family is in that similar excited mode to last year—of expecting the new addition to the family in the New Year and enjoying all the warm fuzziness that comes with the pre-Christmas preparations.

To quote you from one of your earlier letters, bah humbug.

This year I would much rather tell Christmas to go and get stuffed. The thought of decorating my house and putting up my tree turns my stomach.

You see, this time last year I had the best Christmas ever. I have always enjoyed Christmas time and decorating the house and going overboard with cooking and gifts. Love, love, love it. Then in 2011 when I faced my first Christmas after losing Stephen and I was still in a very bad depression, it all cut deep because every time I thought about Christmas I was reminded that a member of my family was missing.

So last year I was totally elated at being able to enjoy Christmas once more. I bought a whole new set of Christmas decorations and totally outdid my house decorating from any previous year, which is quite an achievement.

I was eight months pregnant, expecting our rainbow baby. I still missed Stephen deeply, but I had things to look forward to and not just the ugly cloud of depression hanging over me.

And most of all, last year I just *knew* that I could be happy about Christmas again because I just *knew* that I would never have to go through a Christmas as painful as the year before.

Pause for annihilation of another five tissues.

I am so distraught, Cec. I want nothing to do with Christmas. It distresses me so much that I just want to announce to everyone that Christmas is cancelled until further notice. Also, I never want to be reminded about all the loveliness of babies. I don't want to rob the family of those nice feelings around the time of welcoming a newborn into the family, but right now I don't want anything to do with a family that is expecting a baby.

I am so overwhelmed by this that it is hard for me not to turn these feelings into bitterness. In fact, I can't. I lay in bed for an hour the other night bawling my eyes out and crying out to God not to let me become bitter.

And you know what? It was actually okay with God. He knows how deeply hurt I am and how hard this is for me. And while in practical terms I am finding it very hard not to become bitter about some of these things, the part that is pleasing to God (and of his own doing, might I add) is that my deep desire is *not* to become bitter, because I don't want to move out of love with him or with others.

And this is why I feel such a sense of satisfaction and gladness when I read back over our letters. I can see the journey I have been on. God has brought me to a point where I can understand what it is to be broken in front of him, to know there is no quick fix, and also to know that he doesn't expect me to fix it. He just wants me to love him and to trust him, and I do.

But presently it is very difficult and I feel like I want to run away. The only thing that stops me from doing it is my kids. It's not that I don't love my husband, but I know he'd cope without me for a time. My kids however, would not.

Which I think is sort of what you might have been saying in your last letter. Motherhood is not something we can have a day off from or run away from, and it's hard. It really is a shock when you first move away from your family and you realise that you are responsible for the household, even if it is just you and your spouse. And then the bombshell of responsibility hits when you bring home that first baby from hospital. I remember the first day Michael went back to work after Allison was born and I was freaking out with the responsibility of having a whole other little life to look after;

someone who was totally and utterly reliant upon me for everything.

It's funny how motherhood changes you isn't it? Now I wait to see if the screaming carries on for more than ten minutes or if there is any evidence of blood streaming down the floor. If not, they can deal with it.

Well, almost.

I am so glad that you have been affirmed in your writing, especially with *Invisible*. Nobody likes to be rejected, Cec. Especially when it's something you've poured your heart and effort into as creative people do. When somebody—anybody tells you that they don't like it and don't want to publish it, it's hard not to take it personally because that's exactly what it is—personal—for the author/artist at least.

It does my heart good to hear how God is using your book and your work to touch the lives of others. And I know you've had to work at it. Just as you've had to work at being a wife and mum. And you are a better woman for it.

So I suppose the question is, what is next for Cecily? Any new big ideas on the horizon?

Much love,

Hannah

-18-

Dear Hannah,

There's a reason I left it until this week to answer your letter. I was very nervous about doing it.

Not because of anything you wrote, I should say first up.

No, your letter was great, and it came at a good time because I also had just read back through the whole bath of letters. At some points I cringed, and at other points I laughed but mostly I thought it was interesting to see the journey of grief and friendship we've taken. I think also I've been the one who's stuffed up the most and had to apologise!

The reason I wanted to wait before I wrote was that I thought I might have some bad news for you. News that I really didn't want to write. News that I was hoping wouldn't actually be bad news.

A few months back I found a lumpy bit in my breast. As time went on it seemed to get bigger and finally I thought I shouldn't put it off and went to get a scan and a mammogram.

Let me just say that mammograms are painful. I don't know if they hurt women with less ample bosoms than me, but as you have seen, I am well-endowed in that area and my assets really didn't take too well to being squeezed and then squeezed some more. I actually had bruises for about three days following the test.

So then it was a matter of waiting for results. Which took a long time. And I kept thinking, "Man, I really hope that there is nothing seriously wrong with me, because what the heck am I going to write to Hannah if there is?" Not that I think my well-being is highest on your list of priorities, but because I know how much you've been reacting to the 'C' word this year and how much of an anxiety trigger it's been for you.

And then of course my writer gene obsession thingy kicked in and I thought, "What if I *do* have breast cancer? Wouldn't that be kind of an ironic, but maybe even a fitting ending to this book? We'll have to keep writing because we can't just leave the readers hanging."

I actually was quite nervous about the results although I try not to admit to things like that, and I did my Christmas shopping early *just in case* I had to go have surgery. Which is kind of making light of tragic circumstances, but I am my grandmother's granddaughter and there's nothing like being practical and forward-thinking in life, right?

Anyway. You can probably guess. The results weren't bad. There's nothing to worry about. No surgery or chemo required. I can keep my ample bosoms. And I can write my letter to you without having to worry that you're going to have a panic attack and not be able to continue being a comedian which then would all be my fault.

So with no terrible news and no great disasters on the horizon, I guess life will continue, as it does, with its ups and downs and roundabouts, its hard days and great days and boring days and dirty dishes and glorious sunsets and passing, ticking minutes and hours. These are the bits of life that never make it into the books and the stories. But they're still worth living and worth making the effort for because life isn't just about the triumphs and the tragedies. It's mostly about the trudge and the tread of foot after foot and the daily small decisions to be faithful and loving, as God is to us.

I'm so glad you've come to imbibe more about God's simple love. I use the word 'imbibe' rather than 'know' or 'understand' because it is more than a cerebral assent or a 'finding out'. It's more that when we are so thirsty, all we can do is gulp, forgetting about the 'right' way to hold the cup or worrying about what the people around us will say if we spill drips on the carpet. God really does just want us to love him. And he is so gracious in holding onto us when we have no more energy to hold on to him.

I believe that you'll look back on this period in your life as precious, even though it's been and still is so incredibly hard. Few people can learn these lessons without passing through fire. It sounds schmaltzy, and perhaps it is (if so, shoot me now) but you are being and have been refined more than most of us because of the terrible things that have happened to your babies.

My most heartfelt advice is to continue to be honest in every situation. Our souls thrive on truth-telling and God can handle it, even when we think he can't.

Am I telling you the whole gospel here? Of course I'm not. Who can? Plus I get nervous if I think I'm supposed to say the exact right theological thing at any given point and if there's one thing I really want to avoid sounding like, it's a text book. I had a little giggle that you thought me 'fluffy' back at the beginning of this book. My eight year old had a fluffy 'blankie' right up until last year. Its special talent was getting him to a comfortable, peaceful sleep. In the morning, he woke up happy and refreshed.

Being 'right' and knowing the correct answers is a good thing. But it's not everything. Love is more important. And sometimes loving means saying, "Hey, be a little bit gentle with yourself. You've had a tough time."

I'm going to follow your new path with great interest. I might even come to a show. (And I say that from a default position of being too tight to pay for tickets to pretty much anything.) I think you're going to be great.

As for me, I'll miss our letter writing. But we'll keep up in other ways. You asked me if I have new ideas?

No. No, not really.

I just have the same old idea that I've had for three or four years now, which is to actually succeed at writing these teenage girl novels and, more than that, to earn an income doing it. It's a bit of a slog, but you don't get anything worthwhile without a decent amount of effort, and I'm committed to it, so I'll keep going.

Apart from that, I'll just keep working on family relationships (and by that I mostly mean husband and kids), because if there's one thing I've learned, you can't sit still and assume everything's okay, especially with children coming up to teenage years. I'll continue to work in the community, make fun crafty things, and do the everyday stuff I normally do. I quite like the quiet life.

I do have one dream that might be worth pursuing, I suppose. My husband and I would like to walk the 'Way', the Camino de Santiago, a long path from France to the south of Spain. It can't happen until the youngest is older, obviously, and it can't happen until my books make some money (which means I have to keep working at it) and it might not happen because I've never been a good walker and have flat feet, but it would be amazing, and a massive achievement. Talk to me in five years and I'll tell you how close I am.

That's all from me. It's been great fun. And now, as always, I've got to go pick up my kids and cook dinner.

Thanks for sharing your heart with me.

With lots of love, best wishes and prayers,

Cecily x

-19-

Dearest Cecily,

First of all let me say how glad I am there was nothing of concern with your tests. What an awful time for you and Andrew. And you are not the only one who does very practical things to try and distract you from your anxiety. I cleaned all 160m² of tile grout in our house on my hands and knees with a toothbrush when Stephen was first diagnosed. I'm sure I told myself something about wanting my home to be very clean if we were going to bring a very sick little boy into it.

I, too, am having some mixed feelings about finishing up this particular project of ours. Although as soon as I've written the word 'project' it chafes a little. I suppose in the emotionally detached sense it has been a project. But it's been so much more. And, like you, I have enjoyed reading back over these letters and seeing the way in which our friendship and trust has developed and deepened throughout the course of the year and I am feeling very blessed. In fact I'm tearing up a little, but that's also to do with the fact that I cry at anything at the moment, including the Sorbent™ Toilet Paper commercials.

What you say in your last letter is (once again) absolutely true. Life is very much about the day to day trudge, not just the notable achievements and events. I think this is the thing that has struck me most about writing my own story down and reading the stories of others—it's only the bigger stuff that tends to be recorded, and it's usually all neatly tied up with a big red bow with the hindsight of what has been learned so the reader can go away with some sort of closure. But it really isn't an accurate reflection of what has gone on. A person could sit and read all of our letters in one sitting and walk away without any sense of just how hard the day to day in between has been for both of us. And to be fair, it's not their fault.

Perhaps that is one of the reasons why Jesus is our greatest friend; because he is with us through it all. Even our spouses and dedicated best friends only get glimpses and snapshots of what is happening in our world—our internal world. I think the part I have found so hard about letting Jesus be that friend for me recently is because he is also the friend who could have done something about it all, and chose not to. But instead of chastising me for my difficulty with this, he has sat patiently with me in total understanding and grace and has waited until I have been able to let him in as friend and not just submit to him as Lord. And I think there's a big difference.

I have learned so much about the consequence of our sin. Death. Separation from God. I think I've probably felt it more than the average person. Every day that I am separated from my precious babies is a day of deep hurt and pain. And although Jesus is the only one who has felt the full weight of that curse, I have felt it to be more than I could bear on my own.

The confusing thing was that when the pain was at its most intense, and when my suffering was all-consuming, even the knowledge that one day God will make all things right and that my babies are in safekeeping was not enough. I don't know of many Christians who would admit this. I felt so guilty at the time for feeling that way, but the guilt was all my own. It was not Jesus condemning me for that feeling. He knew and still knows the depth of my hurt— and it is so much more than I can handle, so much more than I was ever created to experience. He doesn't chastise me for that. He loves me through it.

I think there are many Christians who would poo-poo my lack of comfort in the work of Jesus throughout the tough times. But I can't pretend that it was other than what it was.

If I'm really honest, there were times in my deepest sorrow that I wished there was no such person as God, because then I could just move on with my life and put it all behind me rather than holding onto my children as living beings, living somewhere else away from me. There are days when a part of me still wishes that were the case although I think I am just deceiving myself that it would be a better alternative. And they say that belief in God is for the weak minded! Poo-poo to them!

When the most intense grief had passed, and when the unbearable hurt had started to ease (as it always will to some extent, whether or not you are a Christian), I began to return into my right mind (if I ever had such a thing!) And it was in the times when the grief, the mental health complications and the medication started to settle that the work of Jesus made all the difference for me. It meant everything.

Here is the rest of the gospel, dear Cecily, as you are so right in saying. Whilst the suffering and pain has been so very great and has brought me to my knees, I have also never experienced such depth of gratitude and worship and praise for God, in all his persons—praise and worship that has also brought me to my knees in a way I never thought possible.

God, through Jesus indeed has reconciled ourselves to himself so that this awful, gut-wrenching pain of separation is not forever for those who believe. Praise be to God!

As for you and me, I hope that this will not be the last of our letter writing. Perhaps one day when you have achieved what you hope to achieve with your book writing, and you've 'Walked the Way' (which I have to tell you sounds like you want to join some weird sect), and when your children are even closer towards becoming the godly, loving and capable adults you are raising them to be, we will have many more things to talk about it. And I look forward to it all immensely, as well as the day to day blah in-between.

As for my shows, I hope to see you at one of them. Hearing you guffaw and seeing those ample bosoms heave with laughter will do me a world of good. I also hope that we can finally go out for a big piece of chocolate cake afterwards.

With love and blessings abundant, my sister.

Hannah

Blogs & Bits about Grief & friendship

The Top Five Worst Things to say to someone who has lost a baby:

These were things actually said to Michael and/or I after losing our babies:

No. 5 "Oh well, these things happen."

No. 4 "Shhh, stop crying. There's nothing you can do to change it now."

No. 3 "Bad luck just seems to follow you, doesn't it Hannah?"

No. 2 "So why didn't you terminate?"

and... wait for it.... coming in at

No. 1 "Well, there are kids starving on the other side of the world, so it's really not so bad."

I would like to remark here that I am acutely aware that people struggle to know what to say and often are afraid of saying the wrong thing, and that I don't believe that any of the people who made these remarks were being deliberately thoughtless.

For some more information on what can be helpful or unhelpful to say to grieving parents there is a great flyer at http://www.bearsofhope.org.au/a/134.html

Posted 15th June, 2013 on Hannah's Blog *The Bold and the Dutiful* www.47hourswithaprince.com/apps/blog

Lord, this should not be

Written by Hannah Boland, two weeks after Esther was born sleeping.

Lord, this should not be.

I should not have an empty bin to fill.

My bin should be overflowing with dirty nappies

and nursing pads.

I should be waiting until bin night

to see how much I can stash in my neighbour's bin.

Instead, I am left with more than enough space.

Empty, stinky, dirty bin-space.

Lord, this should not be.

I should not want to hide away.

My trips to the shops and trips down town

should be filled with introductions.

I should be showing off my precious girl

to those who have seen my belly grow.

Instead, I am left with a vacant pram.

A neat, clean, useless vehicle.

Lord, this should not be.

I should not have to teach death.

Story times with my children should be

warm and happy.

I should be filling their mind with

delightful and heart-warming concepts.

Instead, I have to explain why our arms are bare again.

Ugly, painful, lonely separation.

Lord, this should not be.

I should not have to avoid

a room in my home.

I had the final touches ready to put up in the nursery.

I should be teetering on a ladder and

rebuked by my husband for doing too much.

Instead, I am fighting back tears because I have

plain walls.

Bland, stark, undecorated walls.

Lord, this should not be.

I should not be ending every day with a

pool on my pillow.

My nights should be sleepless and restless for sure.

I should be feeding and soothing and debating

whose turn it is with my husband.

Instead, I am glued to my bed with two empty tissue boxes.

Countless, salty, uncontrollable tears.

Lord, this should not be.

I should not be afraid to

spend time with my friends.

I am petrified that the focus is me.

I should be serving, loving, caring,

and a pleasure to spend time with.

Instead, I dissolve into heartache from the

slightest compassionate glance.

Uncontrollable, unmeasurable, unwanted pain.

Lord, this should not be.

I should not and no one should.

But I remember how wicked we have been.

I'm Sad and I Need Cake

We should have loved you and trusted you

at the beginning.

Instead, you had to become a source of joy and peace

amongst the turmoil.

Awaited, anticipated, life-giving hope.

Cecily's Delectable Dairy-free Treats

Best if you have a Thermomix™ but a food processor (or a knife!) will still work.

Magic Bean Cake (gluten, dairy and soy free)

This really is a magic cake. You certainly wouldn't know it was gluten free from the taste. I make this once a week for my kids.

Ingredients

180g sugar *or whatever healthy equivalent you choose*

400g can of cannellini beans

1 tbsp vanilla essence

125g Nuttelex™ *or butter or coconut oil or whatever fat you prefer*

5 eggs

½ teaspoon of bicarb

1 tsp baking powder

¼ tsp salt

70g cocoa

(Method over page)

Method

1. Whizz together sugar, beans, vanilla essence and Nuttelex™ on speed 6 of your Thermomix™ until combined (or just get it going real good in your food processor. It needs to look smooth and whipped by the end).
2. Add the eggs, bicarb, baking powder, salt and cocoa and whizz again until the whole thing is smooth and looks like a cake mix should!
3. Pour into a prepared cake tin or cupcake liners and bake at 180⁰C until the cake bounces back or a skewer comes out clean. (The time varies depending on if you do cake or cupcakes.)

Pretty Nice Brownies

I actually invented this one. When I consider that most of my 'lets-just-try-it' recipes are dodgy at best, to get an actual, reproducible batch of yummy brownies was a big deal.

Ingredients

200g almonds

8-10 dates

200g Nuttelex™ *or butter or your preferred fat*

¾ cup *sugar or equivalent sweetener*

60g cocoa

2 eggs, beaten

1 tsp baking powder

60g Teff flour *or any other gluten free flour. Millet or brown rice flour also work well.*

Method

1. Grind almonds together with dates until they resemble almond meal. Set aside.
2. Melt Nuttelex™ with sugar and add cocoa.
3. Add eggs and baking powder and mix.
4. Combine this with the almond and date mixture as well as the flour.
5. Pour into a brownie tin and bake in a moderate oven until the brownies are set.

Coconut Milk Ice-cream

This is the easiest ice cream ever.

Ingredients

2 eggs

400g tin coconut cream

1 tsp vanilla essence

80g sugar *or more if you like a very sweet ice-cream*

Method, if using a Thermomix™

1. Beat the eggs, coconut cream, vanilla essence and sugar together in the Thermomix™.

2. Cook for 8 minutes at 80°C on speed 4. Congratulations. You have just made crème anglaise. Refrigerate until cold.
3. Churn in an ice-cream maker until set.

(Stovetop directions over page)

Stovetop directions for those without a Thermo

1. On the stovetop make the custard by beating ingredients together and then stirring constantly over a low heat until the mixture thickens enough to cover the back of a wooden spoon.
2. Refrigerate custard until cold, then churn in an ice-cream maker until set.

If you have no ice-cream maker, pour into a container and freeze until partially set. Then whip it up with beaters so it's smooth. Freeze again. Repeat a few times until the ice-cream is smooth.

www.ingramcontent.com/pod-product-compliance
Lightning Source LLC
Chambersburg PA
CBHW032101080426
42733CB00006B/369